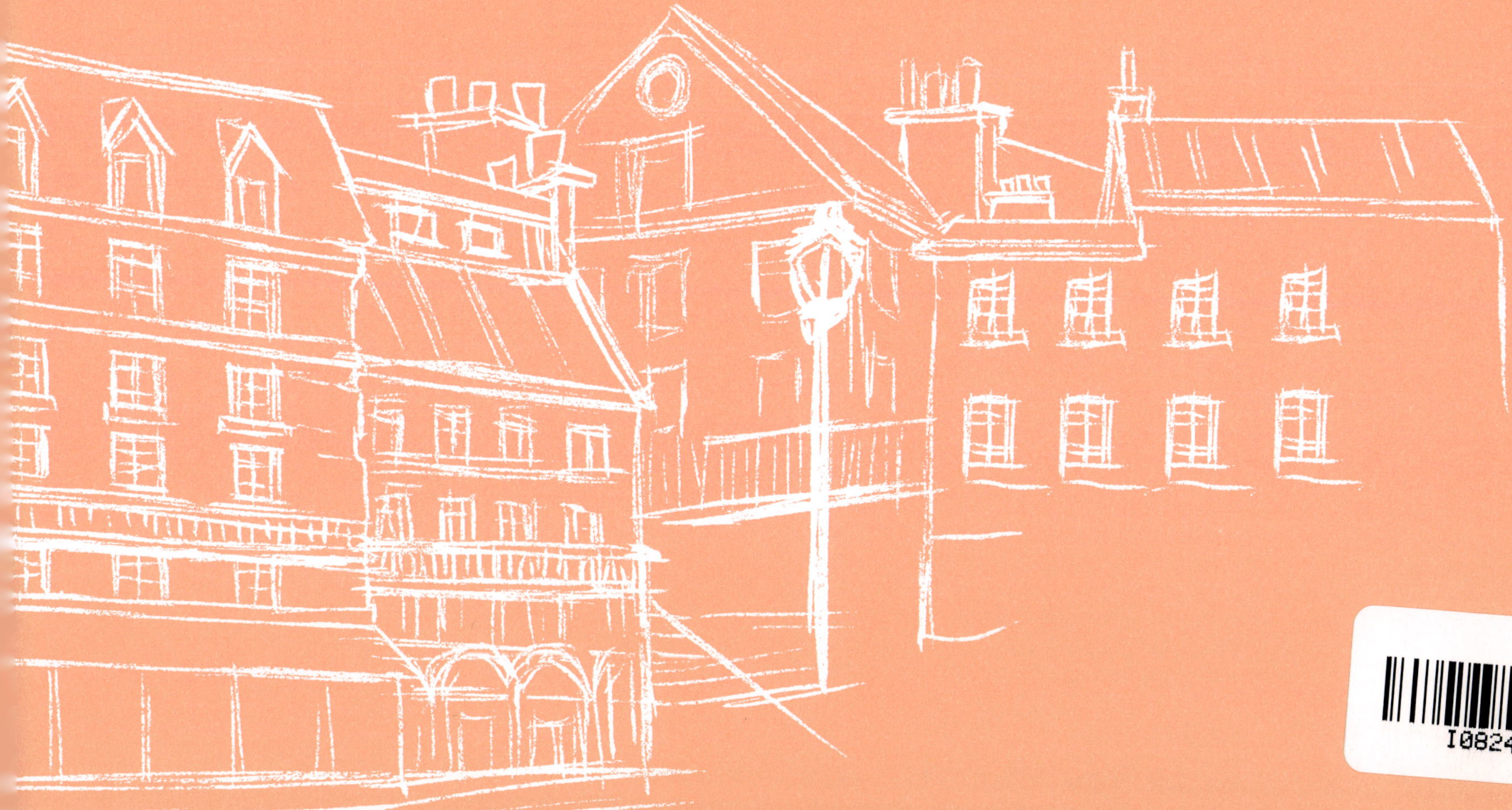

I0824057

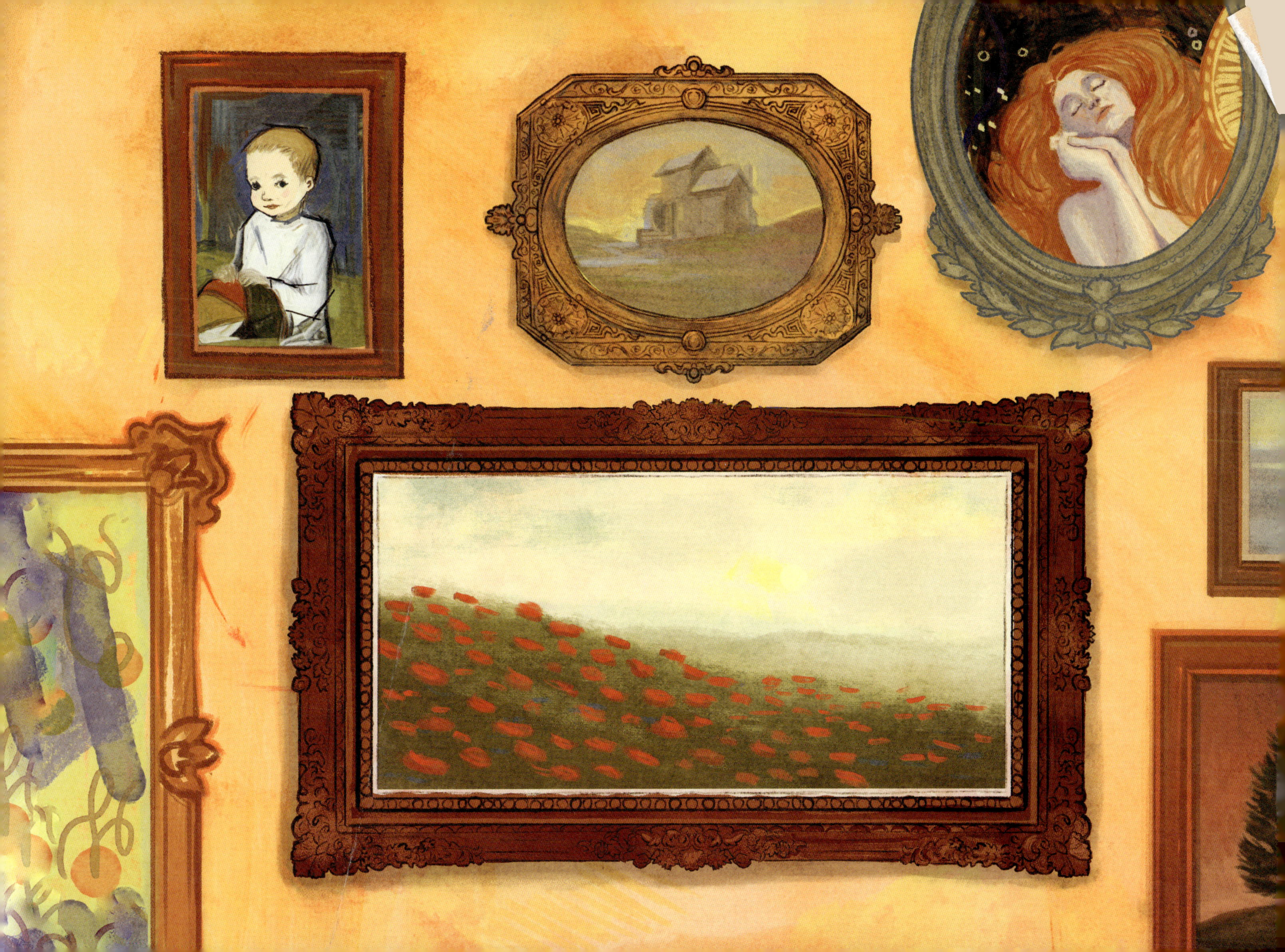

The Spy in the Museum

How Rose Valland Saved Art from the Nazis

Written and illustrated by
Erin McGuire

Beach Lane Books New York Amsterdam/Antwerp London Toronto Sydney/Melbourne New Delhi

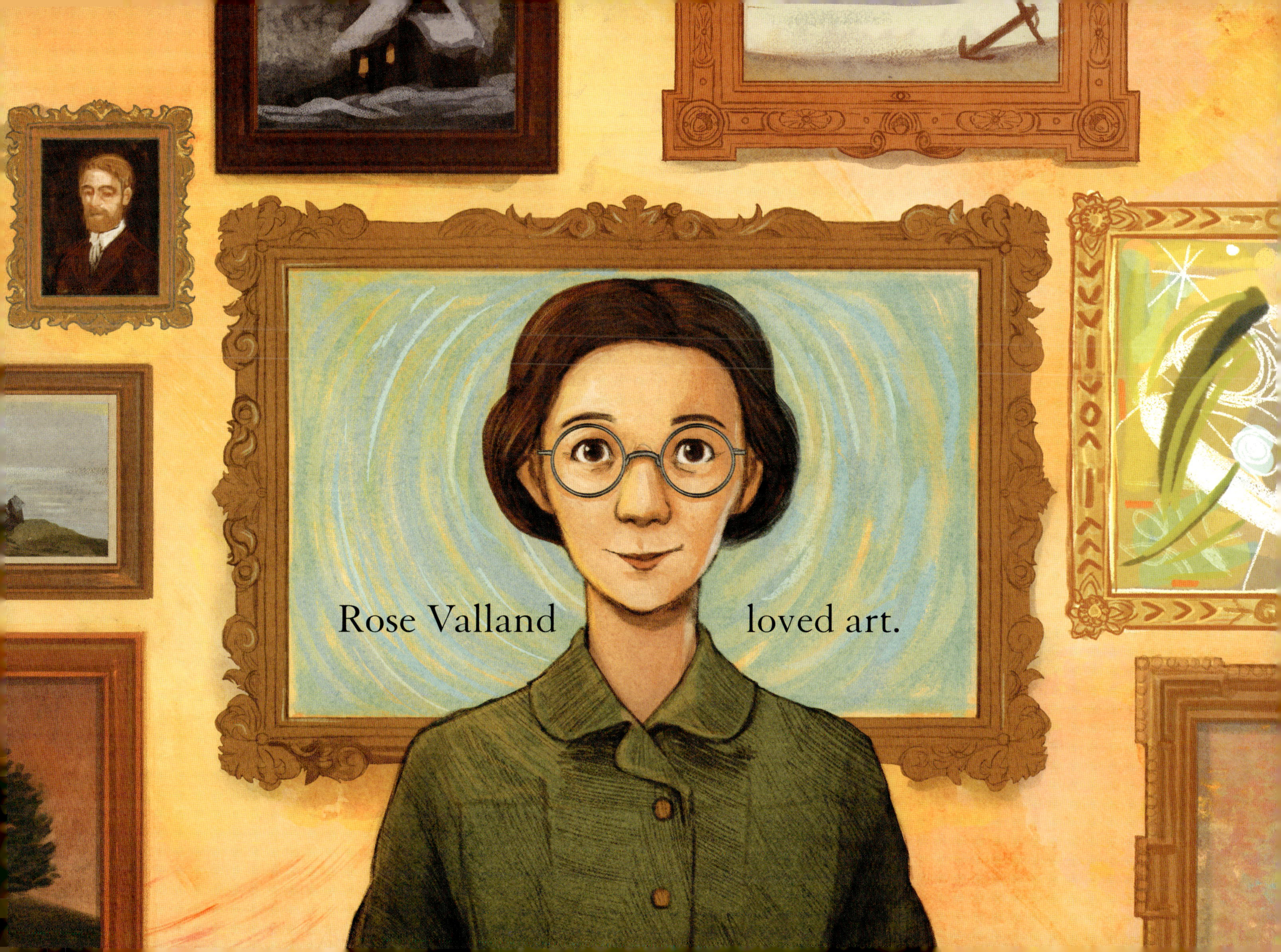

Rose Valland loved art.

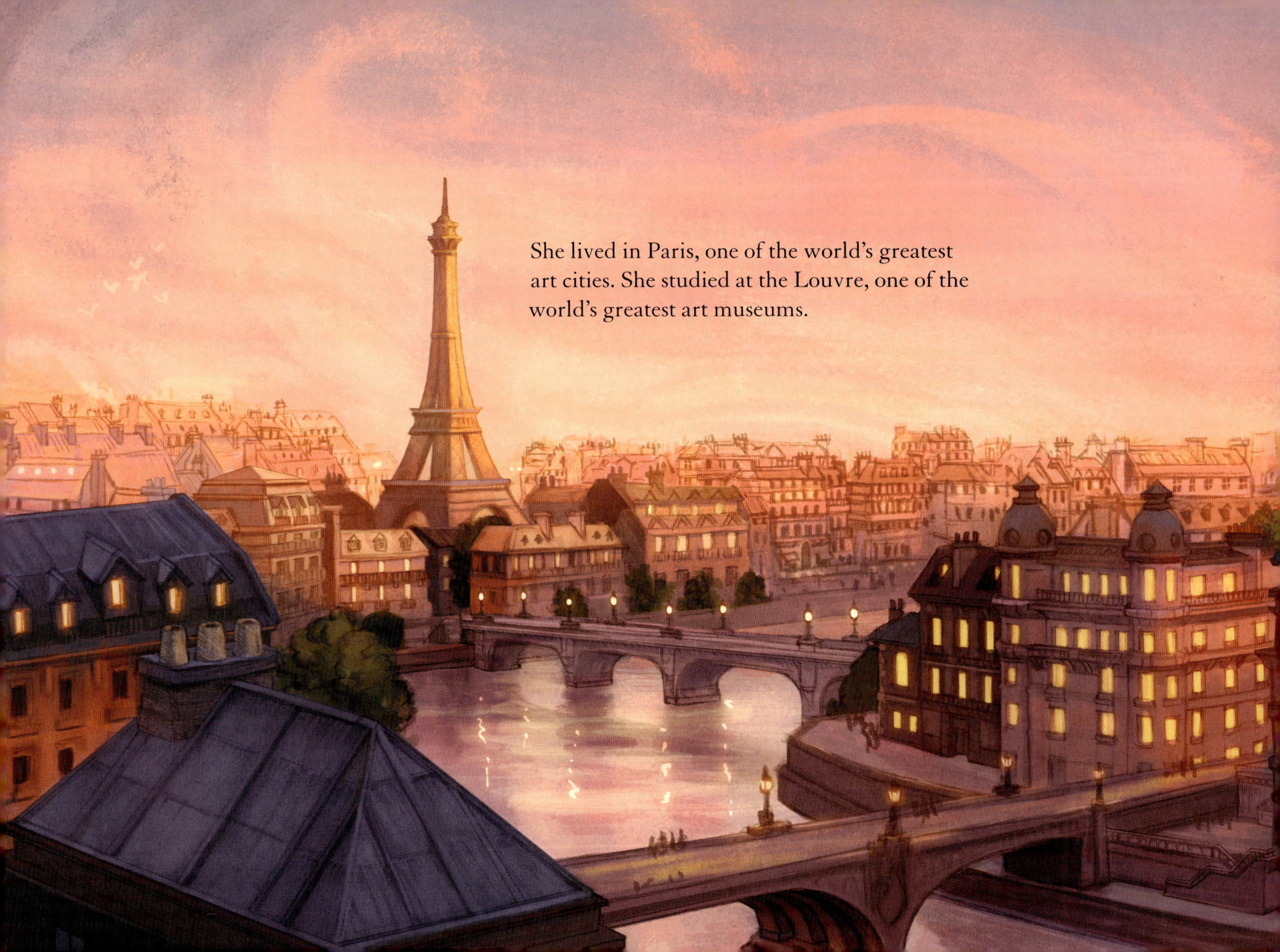

She lived in Paris, one of the world's greatest art cities. She studied at the Louvre, one of the world's greatest art museums.

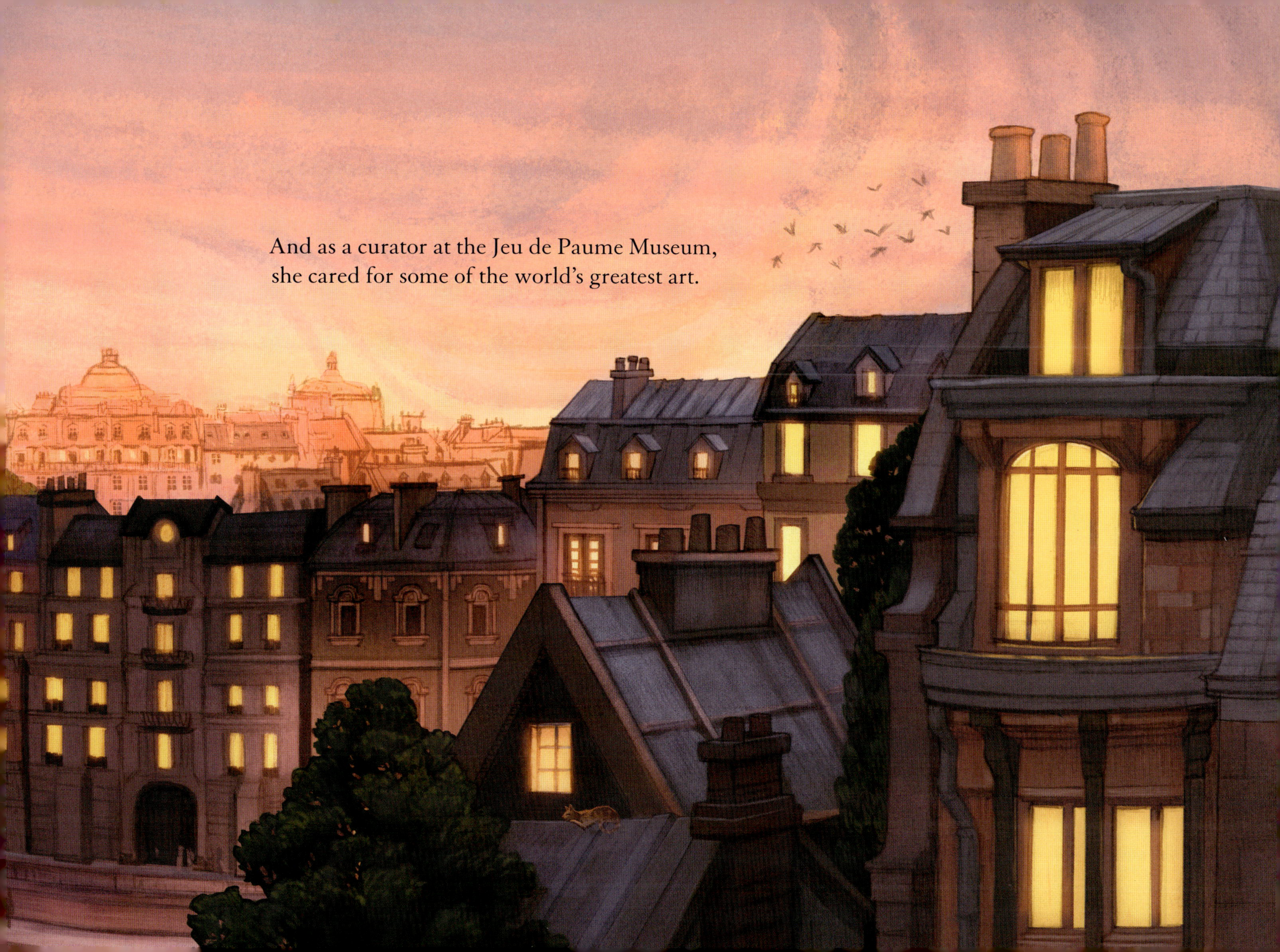

And as a curator at the Jeu de Paume Museum, she cared for some of the world's greatest art.

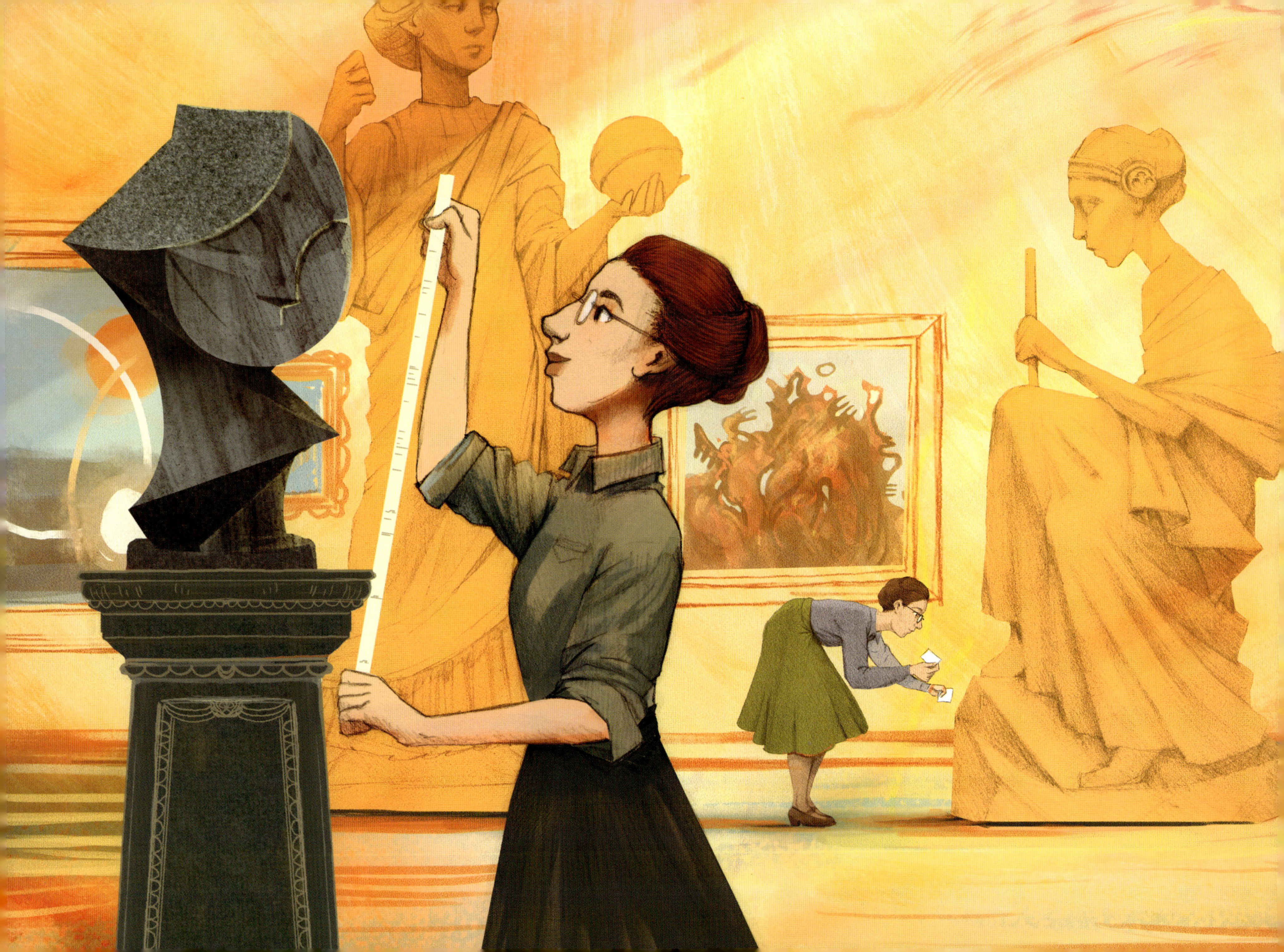

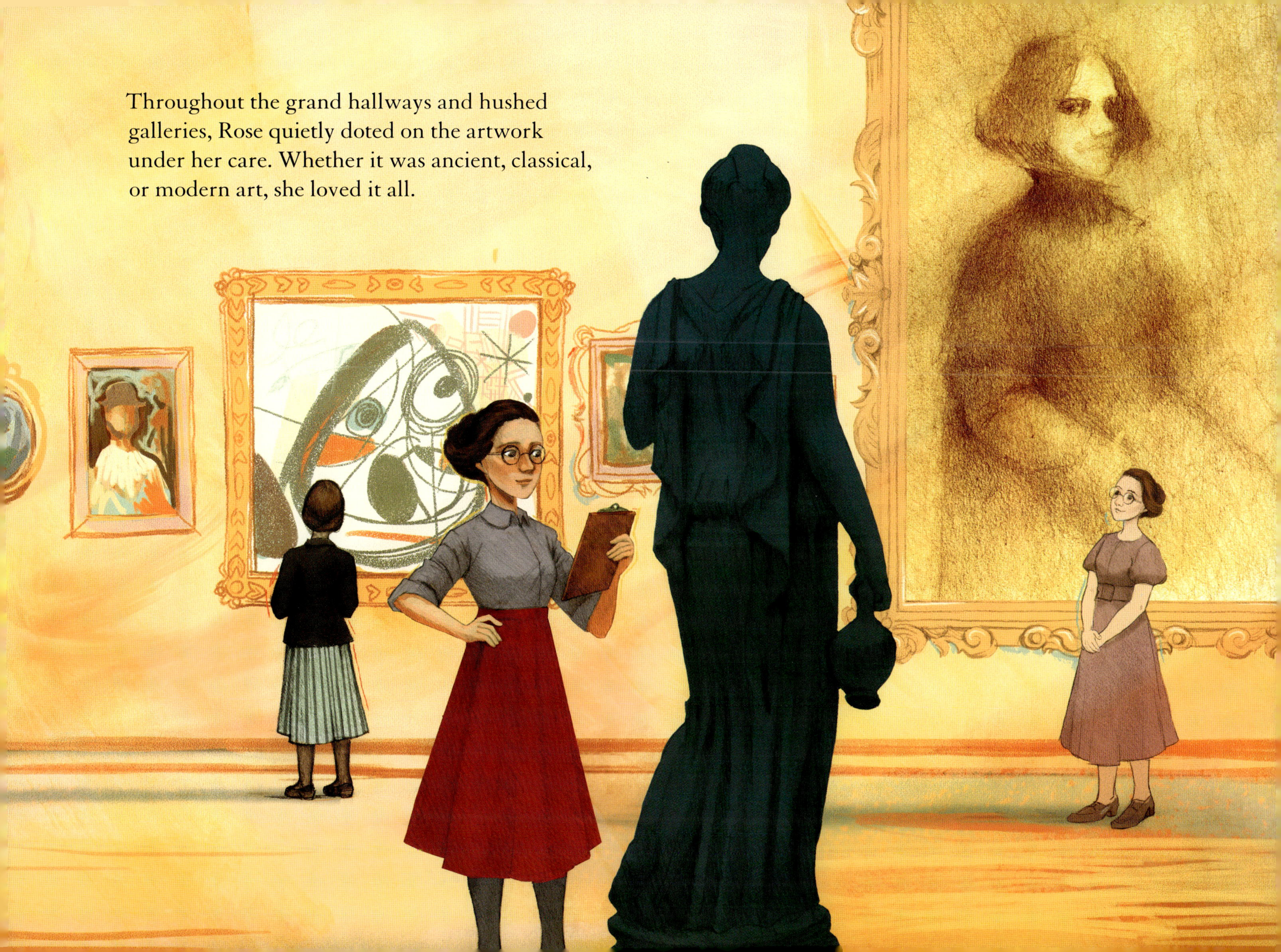

Throughout the grand hallways and hushed galleries, Rose quietly doted on the artwork under her care. Whether it was ancient, classical, or modern art, she loved it all.

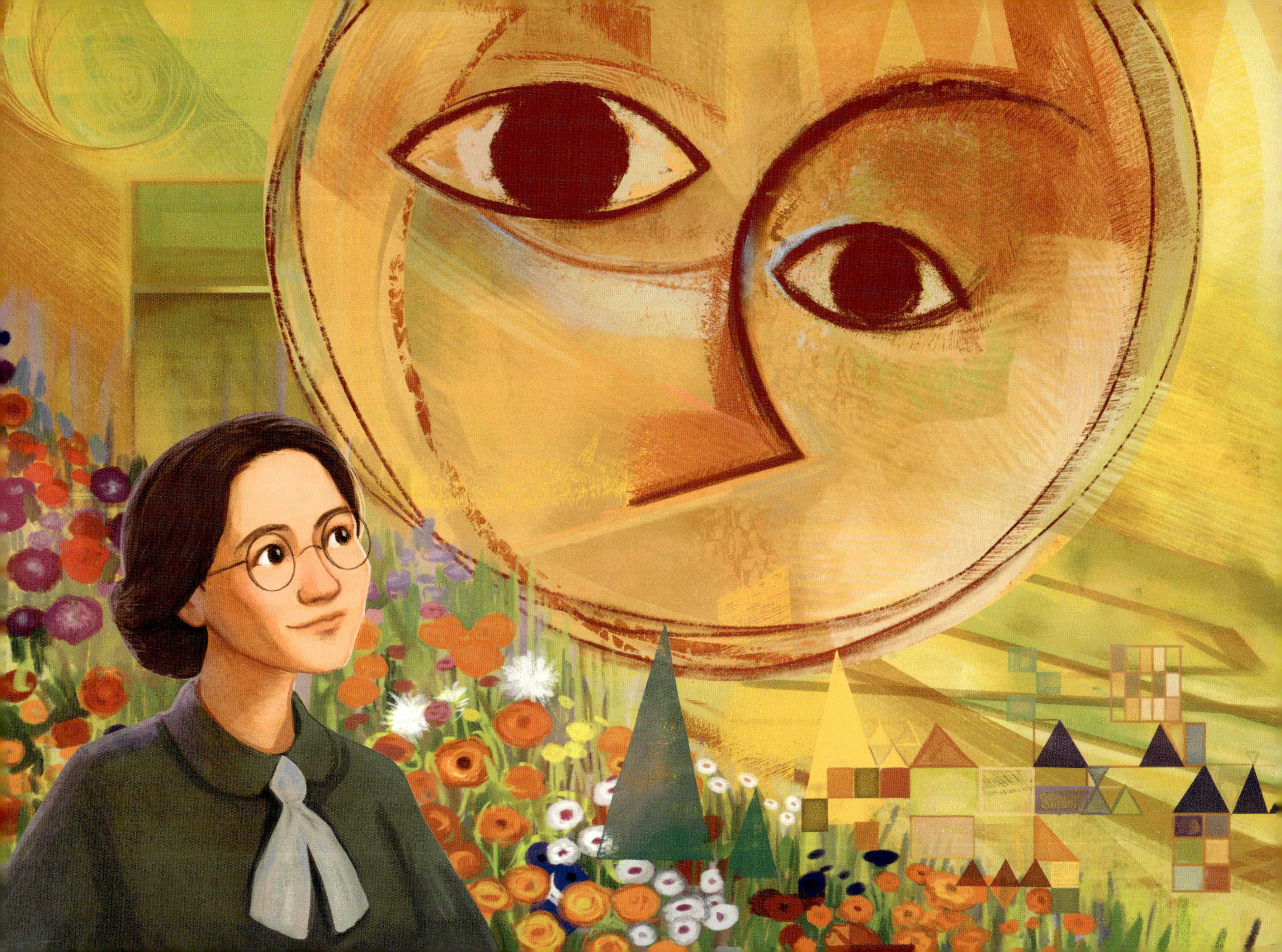

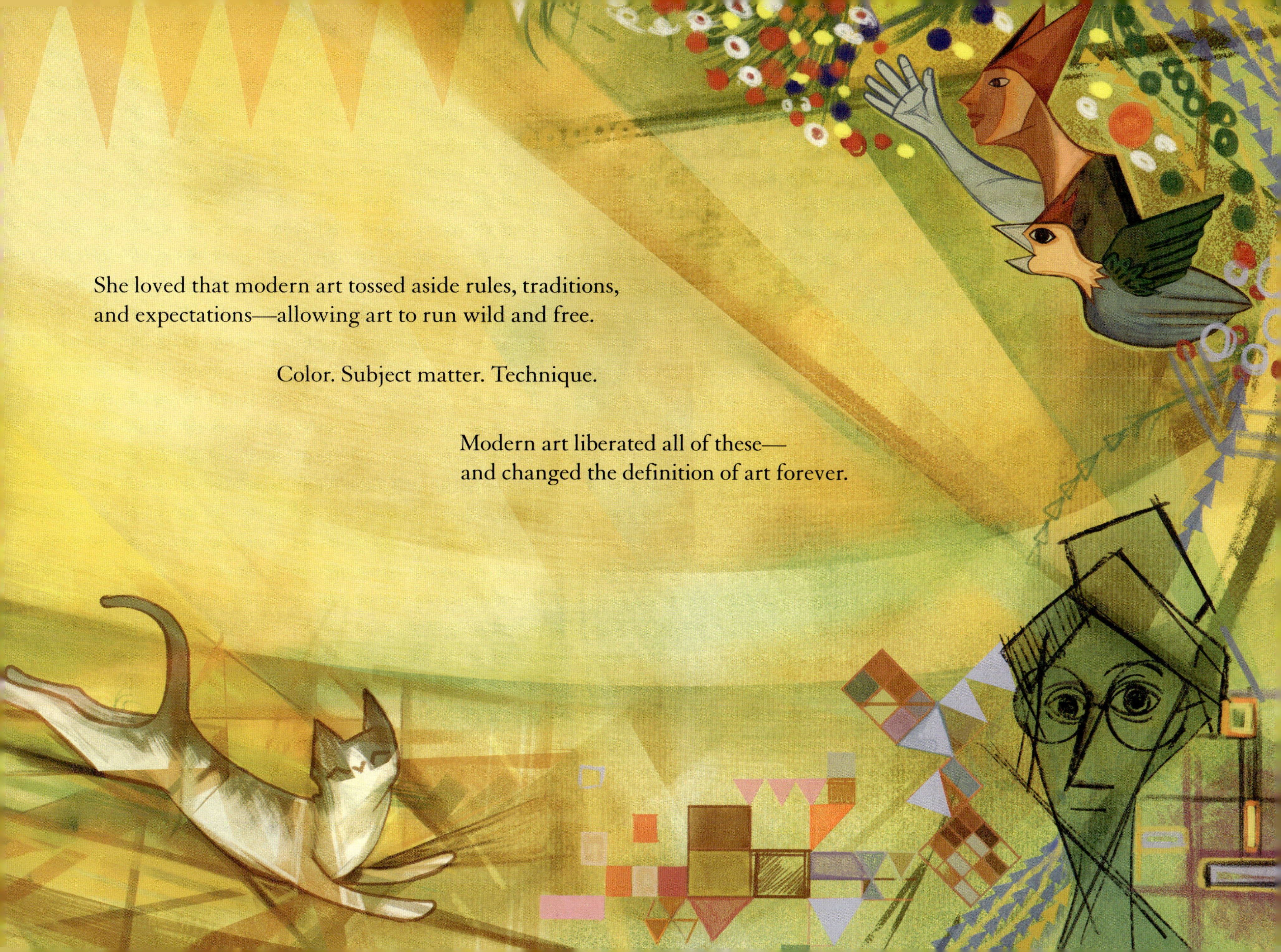

She loved that modern art tossed aside rules, traditions, and expectations—allowing art to run wild and free.

Color. Subject matter. Technique.

Modern art liberated all of these—
and changed the definition of art forever.

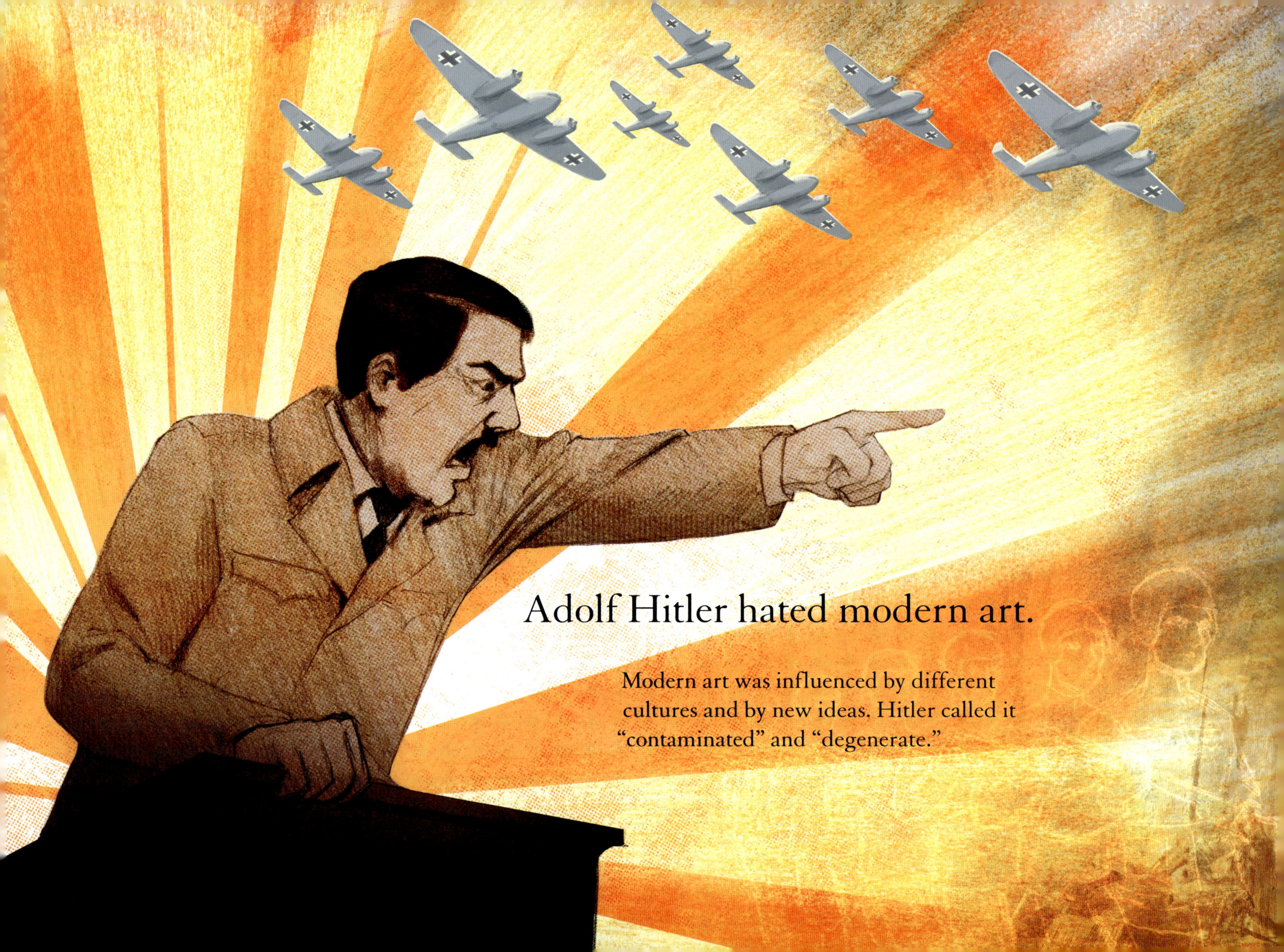

Adolf Hitler hated modern art.

Modern art was influenced by different cultures and by new ideas. Hitler called it "contaminated" and "degenerate."

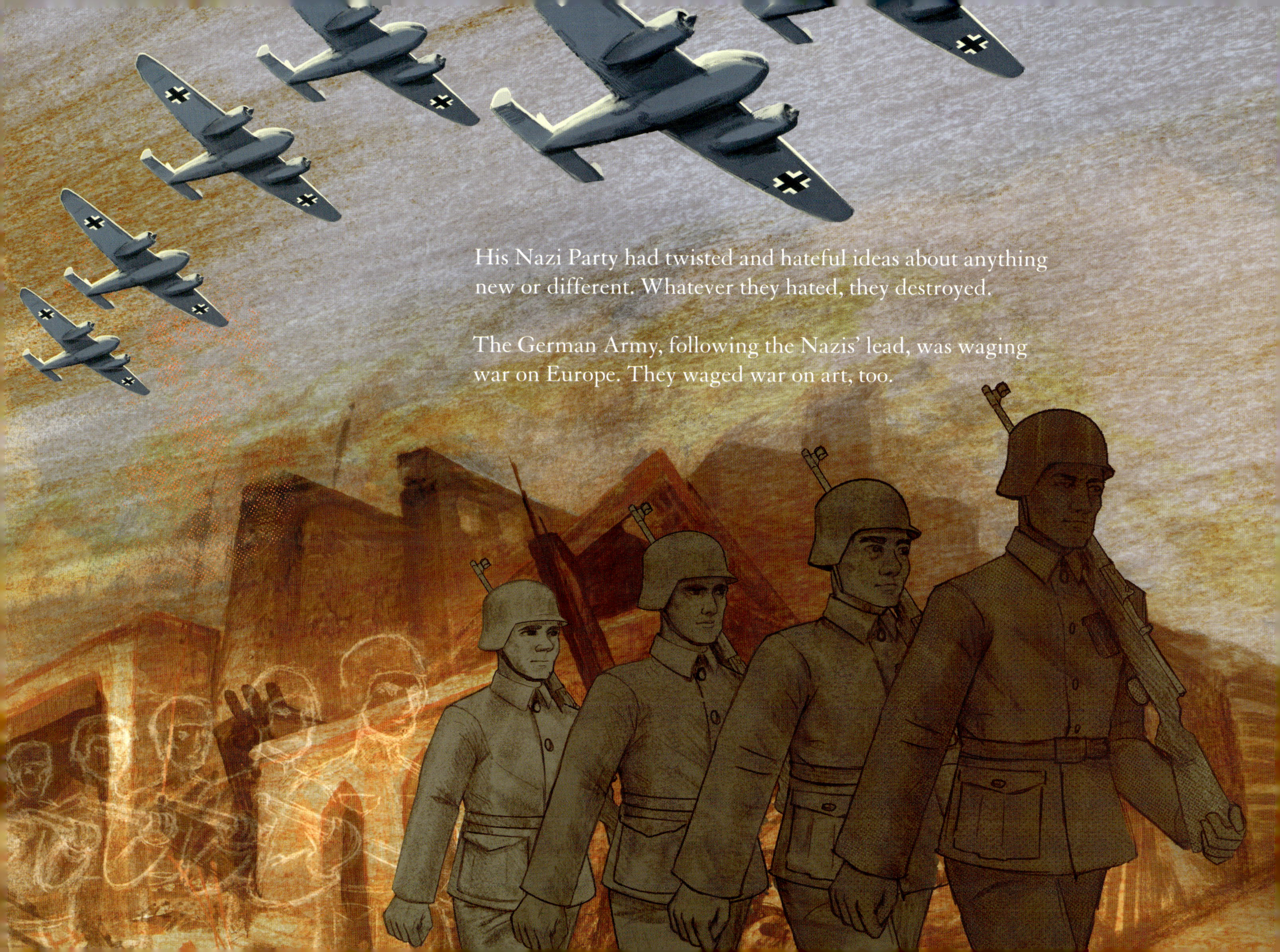

His Nazi Party had twisted and hateful ideas about anything new or different. Whatever they hated, they destroyed.

The German Army, following the Nazis' lead, was waging war on Europe. They waged war on art, too.

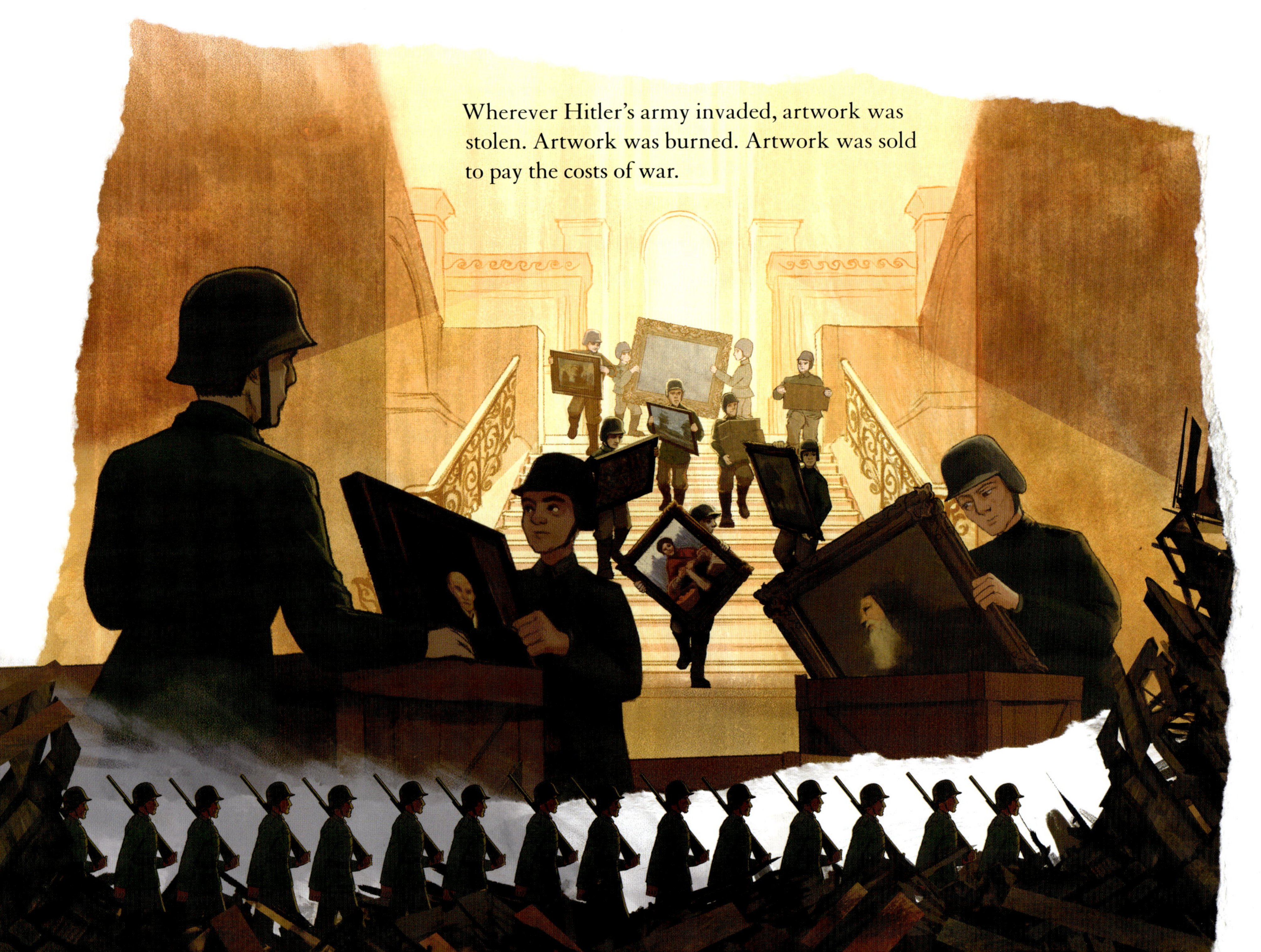

Wherever Hitler's army invaded, artwork was stolen. Artwork was burned. Artwork was sold to pay the costs of war.

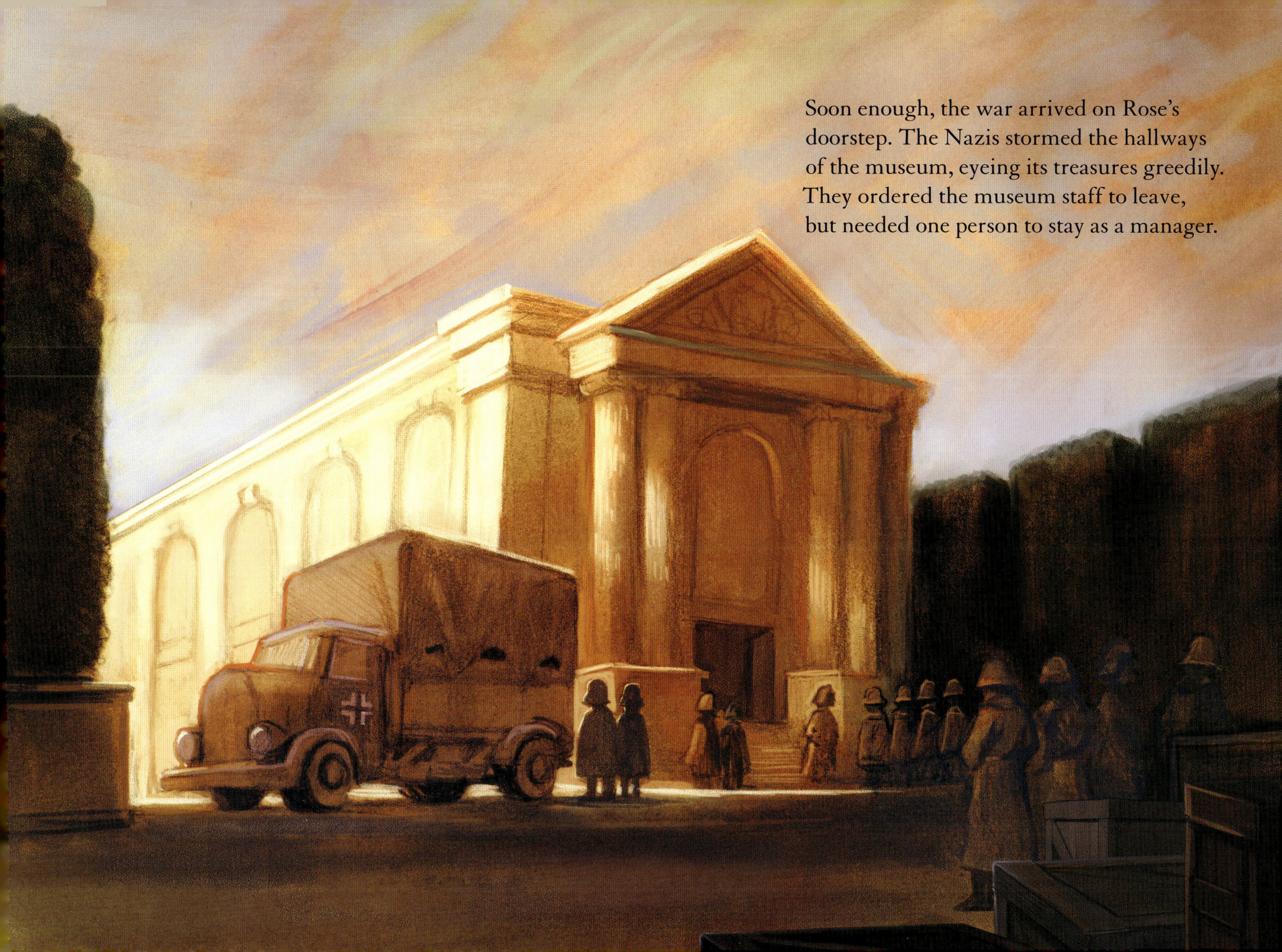

Soon enough, the war arrived on Rose's doorstep. The Nazis stormed the hallways of the museum, eyeing its treasures greedily. They ordered the museum staff to leave, but needed one person to stay as a manager.

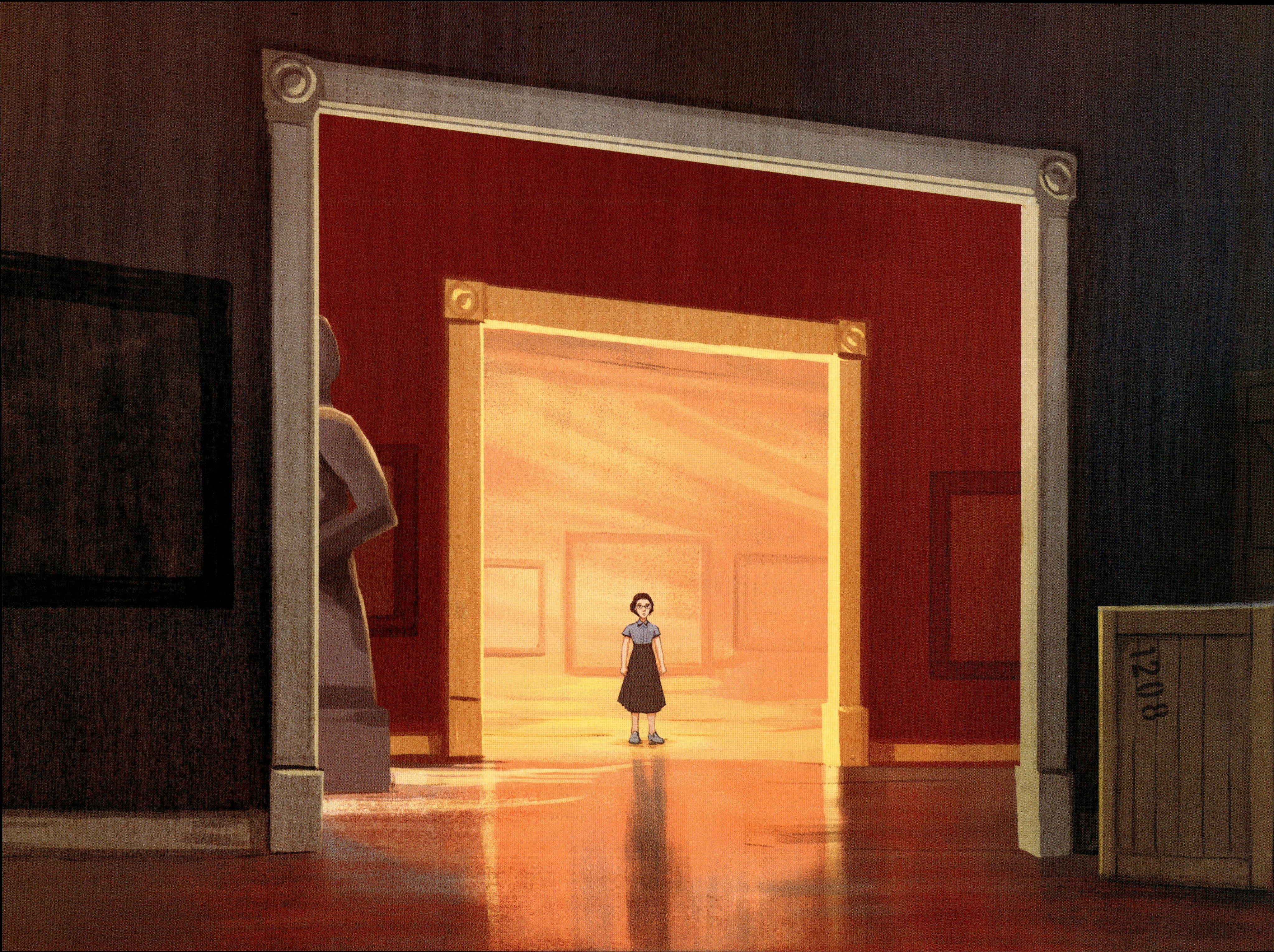
1208

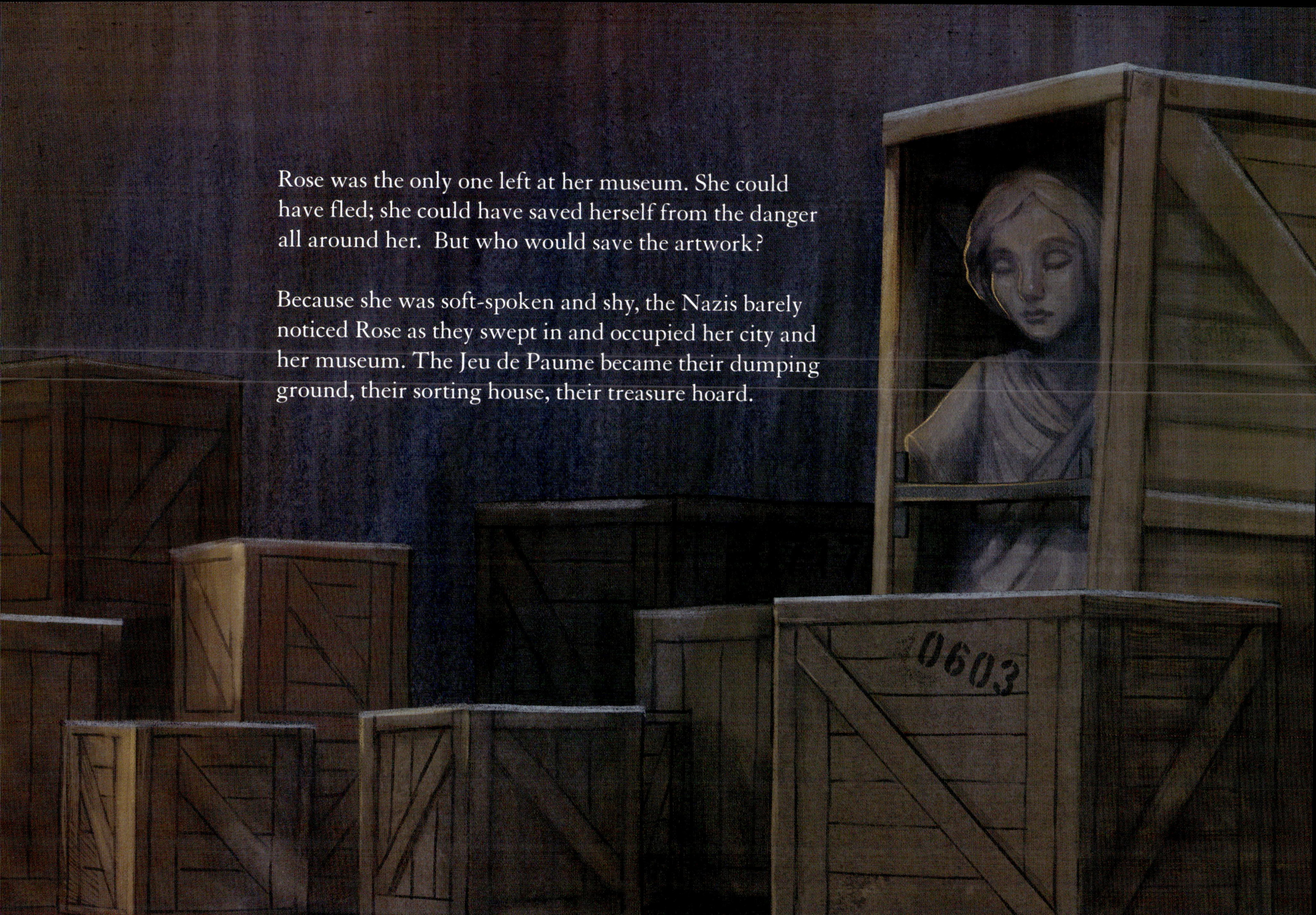

Rose was the only one left at her museum. She could have fled; she could have saved herself from the danger all around her. But who would save the artwork?

Because she was soft-spoken and shy, the Nazis barely noticed Rose as they swept in and occupied her city and her museum. The Jeu de Paume became their dumping ground, their sorting house, their treasure hoard.

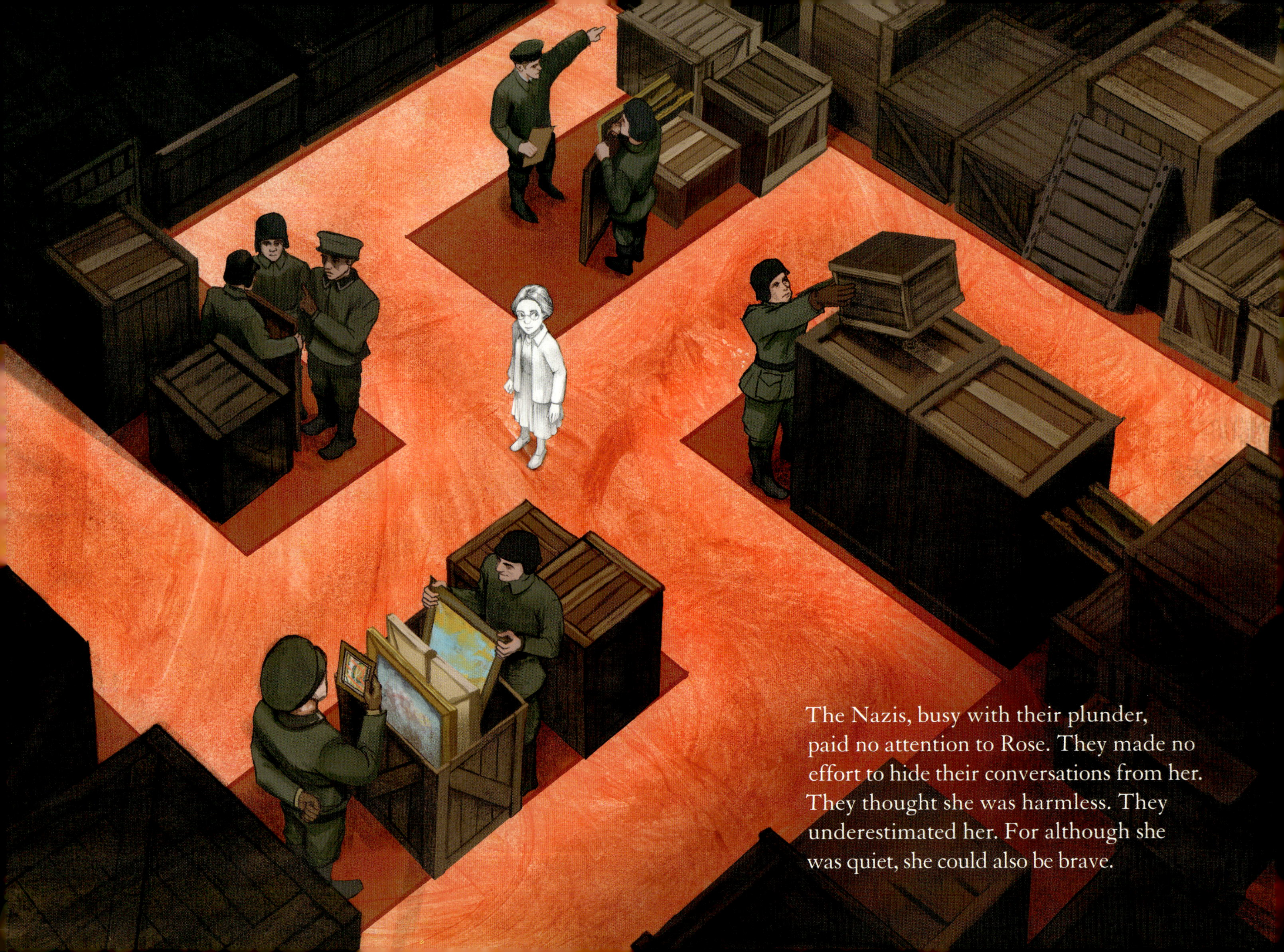

The Nazis, busy with their plunder, paid no attention to Rose. They made no effort to hide their conversations from her. They thought she was harmless. They underestimated her. For although she was quiet, she could also be brave.

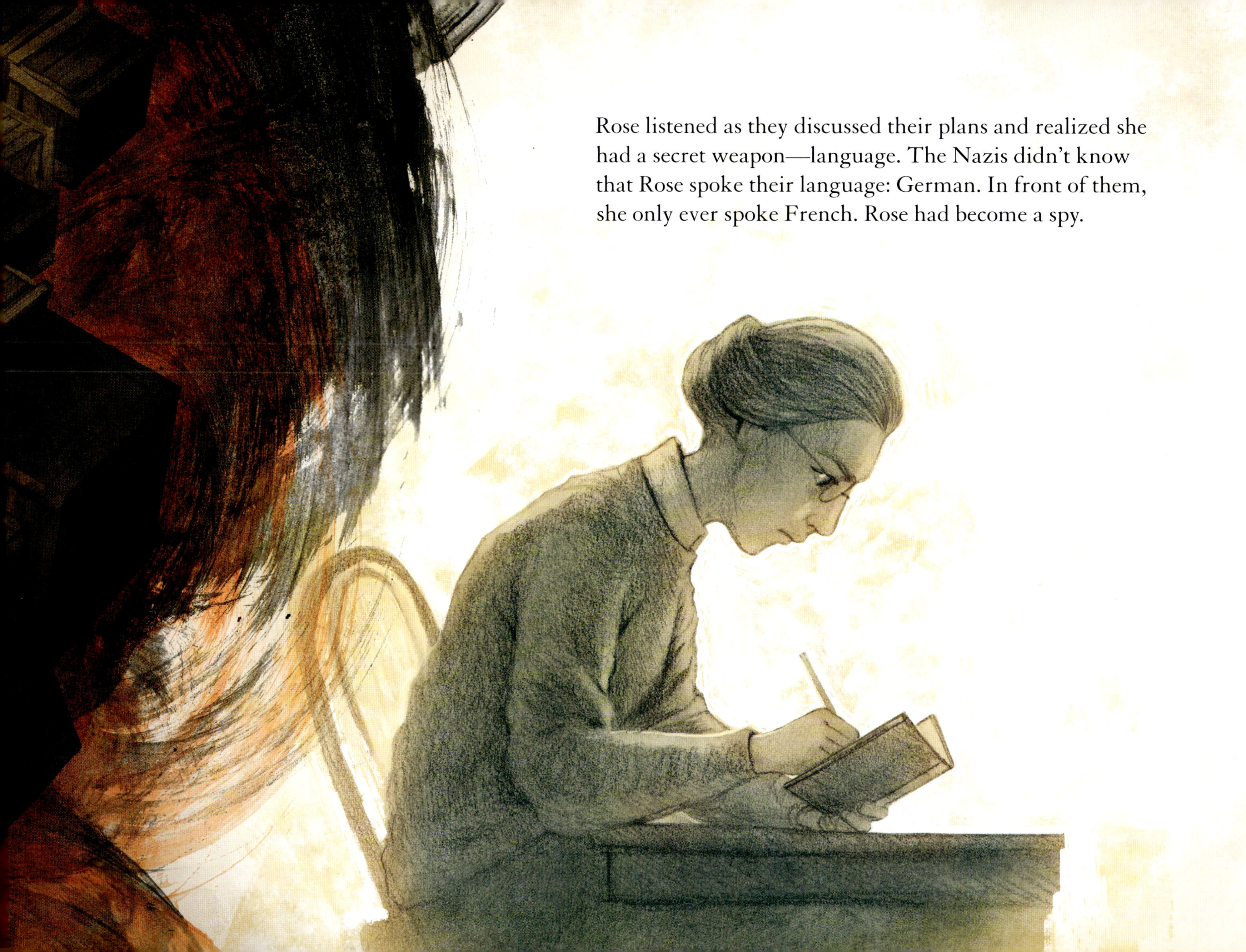

Rose listened as they discussed their plans and realized she had a secret weapon—language. The Nazis didn't know that Rose spoke their language: German. In front of them, she only ever spoke French. Rose had become a spy.

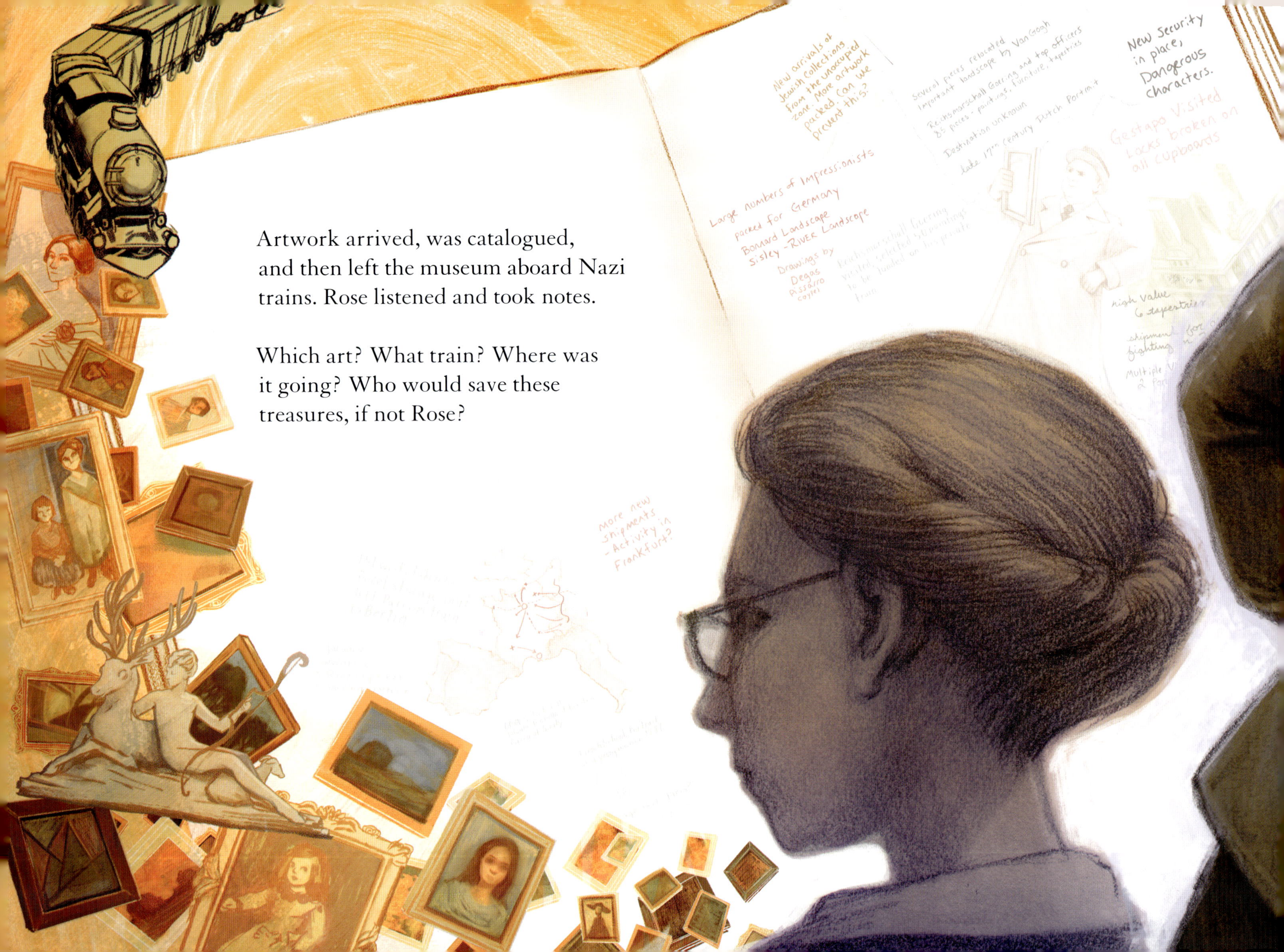

Artwork arrived, was catalogued, and then left the museum aboard Nazi trains. Rose listened and took notes.

Which art? What train? Where was it going? Who would save these treasures, if not Rose?

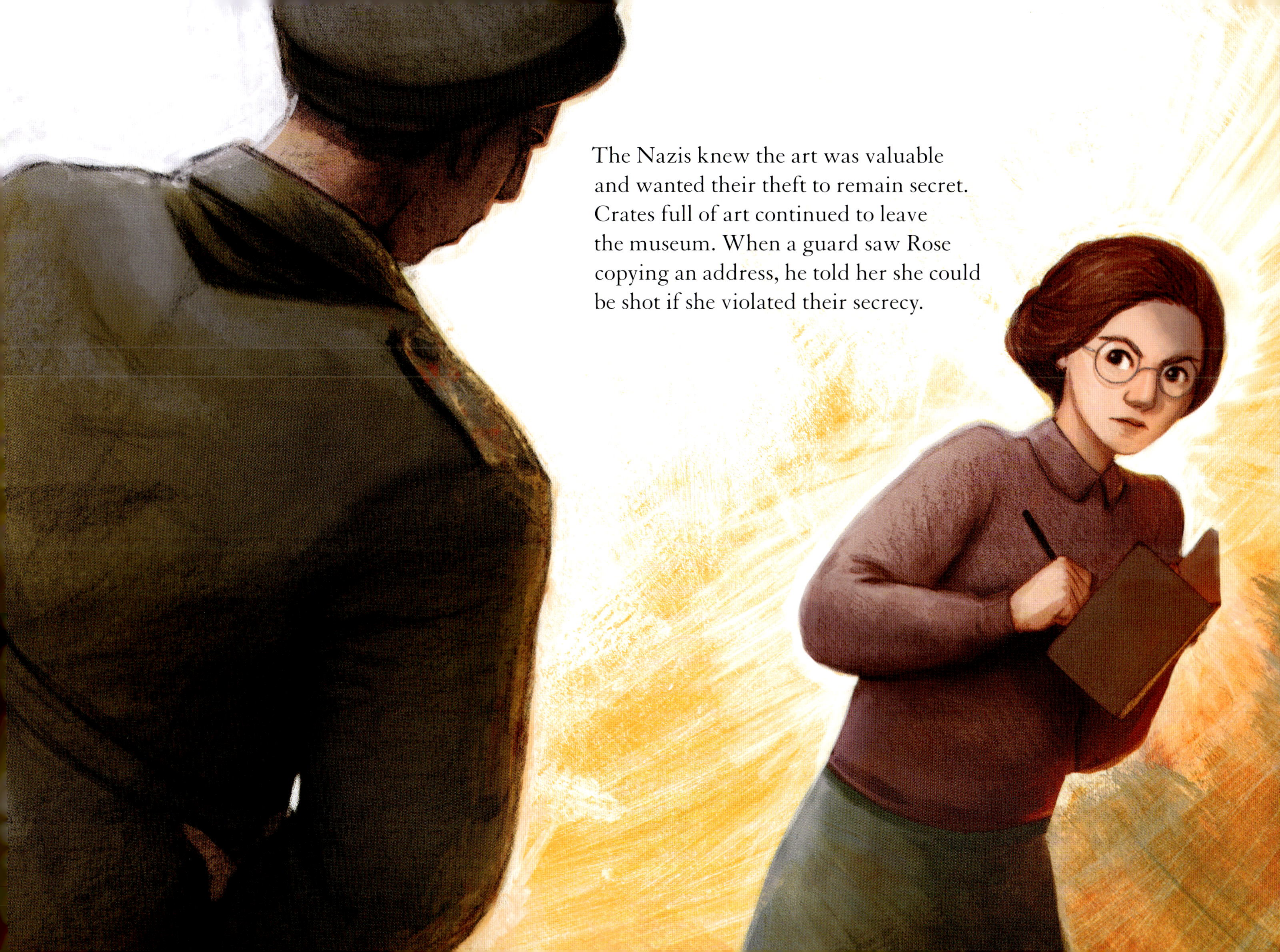

The Nazis knew the art was valuable and wanted their theft to remain secret. Crates full of art continued to leave the museum. When a guard saw Rose copying an address, he told her she could be shot if she violated their secrecy.

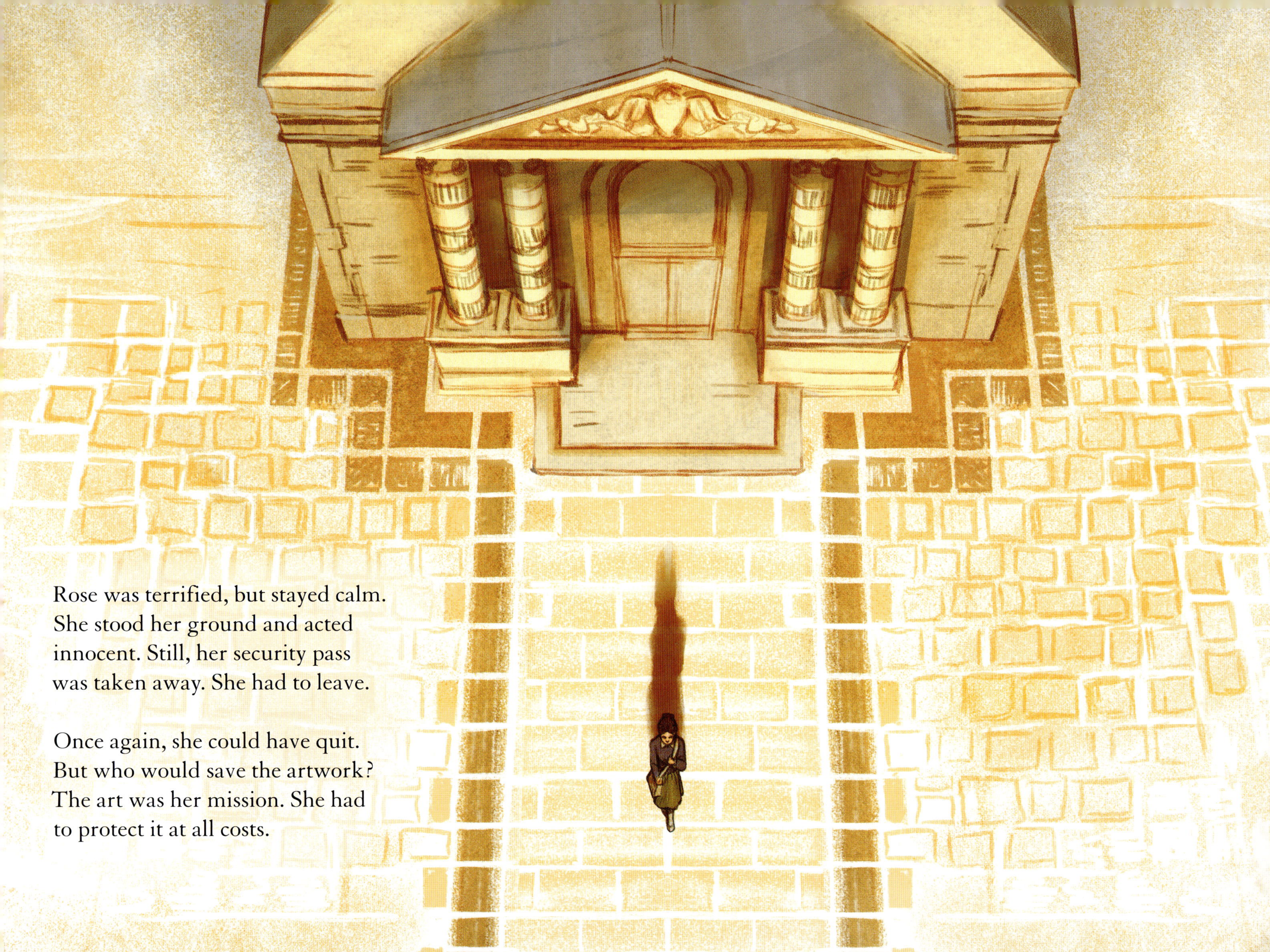

Rose was terrified, but stayed calm. She stood her ground and acted innocent. Still, her security pass was taken away. She had to leave.

Once again, she could have quit. But who would save the artwork? The art was her mission. She had to protect it at all costs.

After a few days, new guards were posted at the museum. Rose talked her way back in.

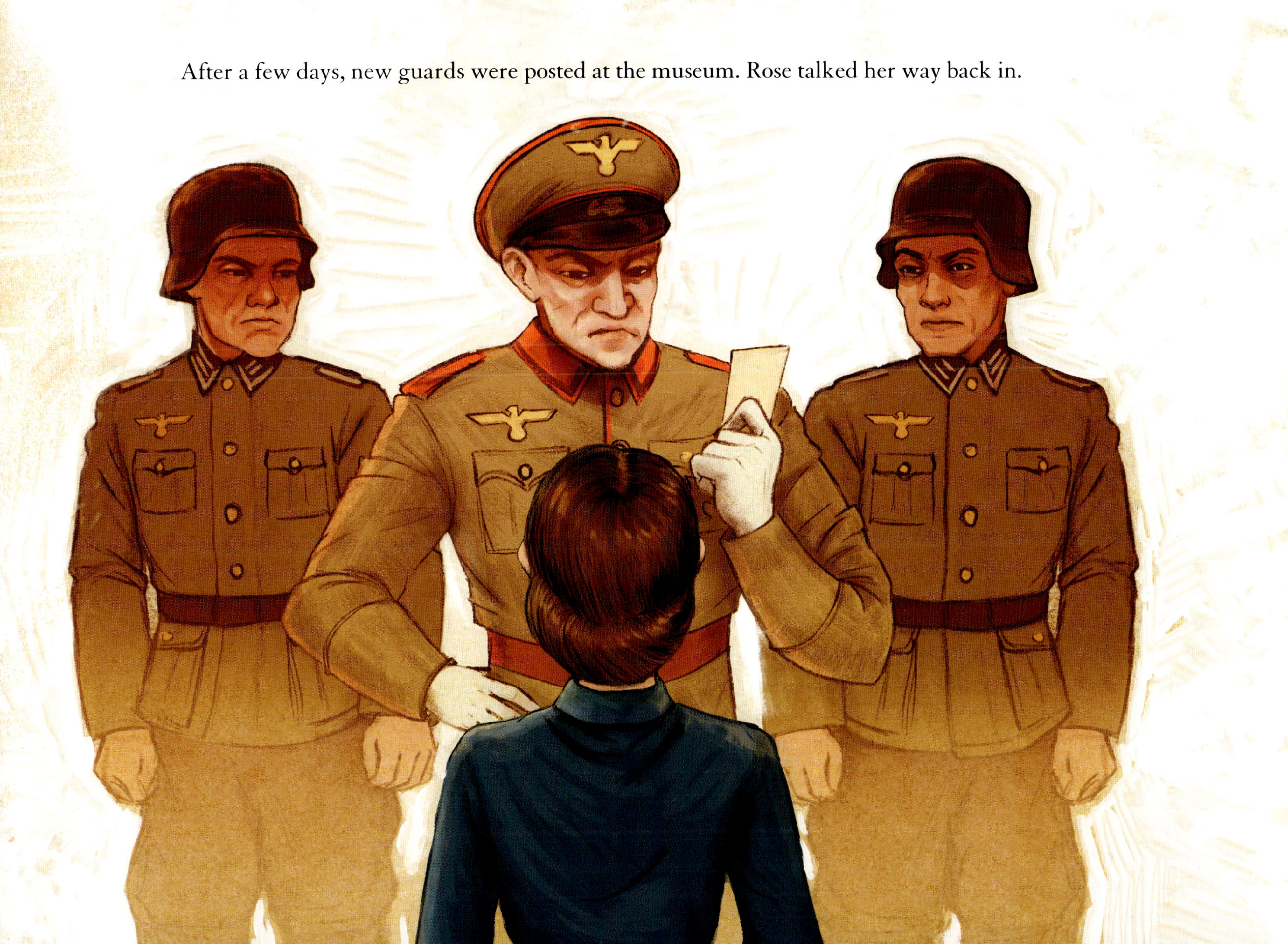

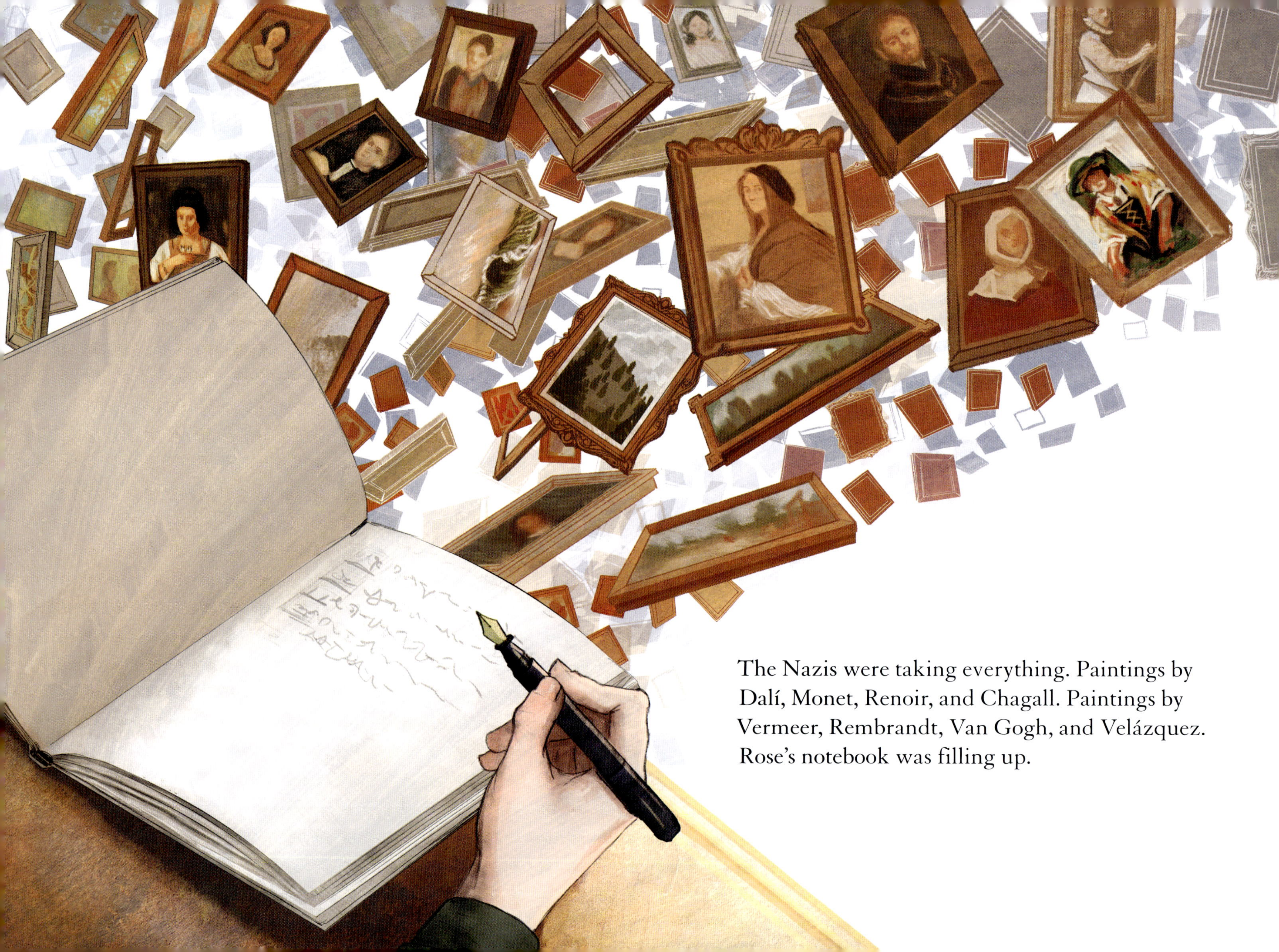

The Nazis were taking everything. Paintings by Dalí, Monet, Renoir, and Chagall. Paintings by Vermeer, Rembrandt, Van Gogh, and Velázquez. Rose's notebook was filling up.

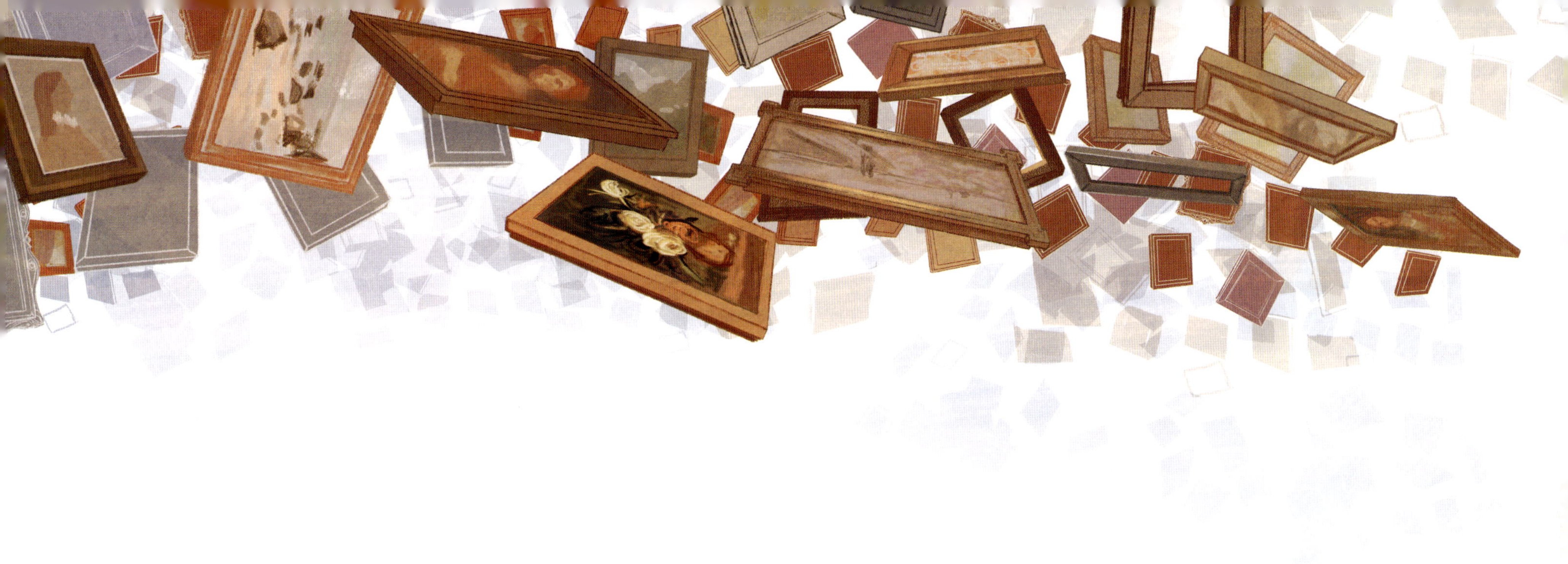

Again and again, they tried to dismiss her, to threaten her, to kick her out. She kept finding excuses to return.

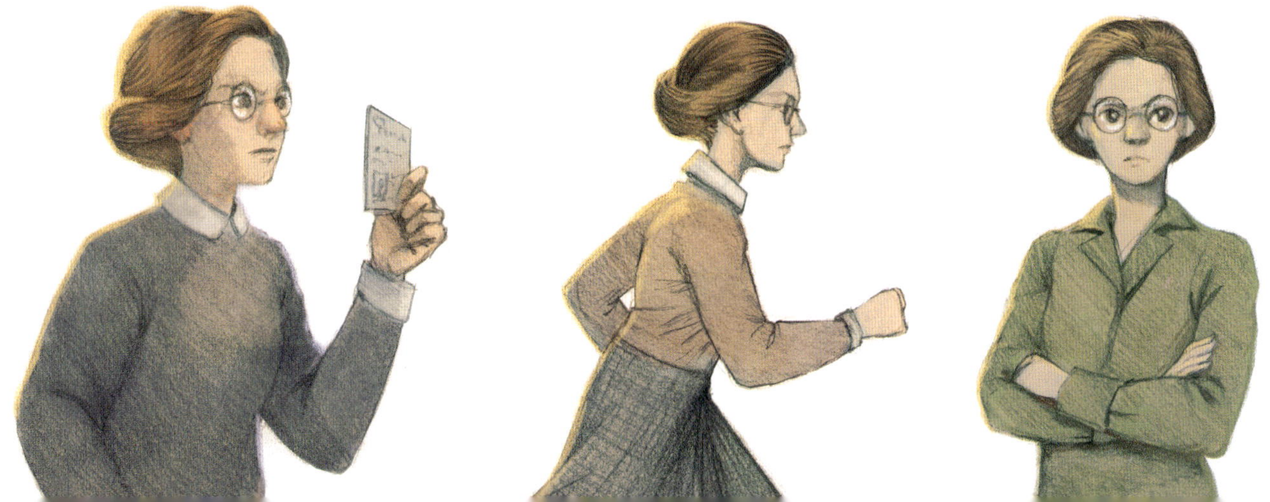

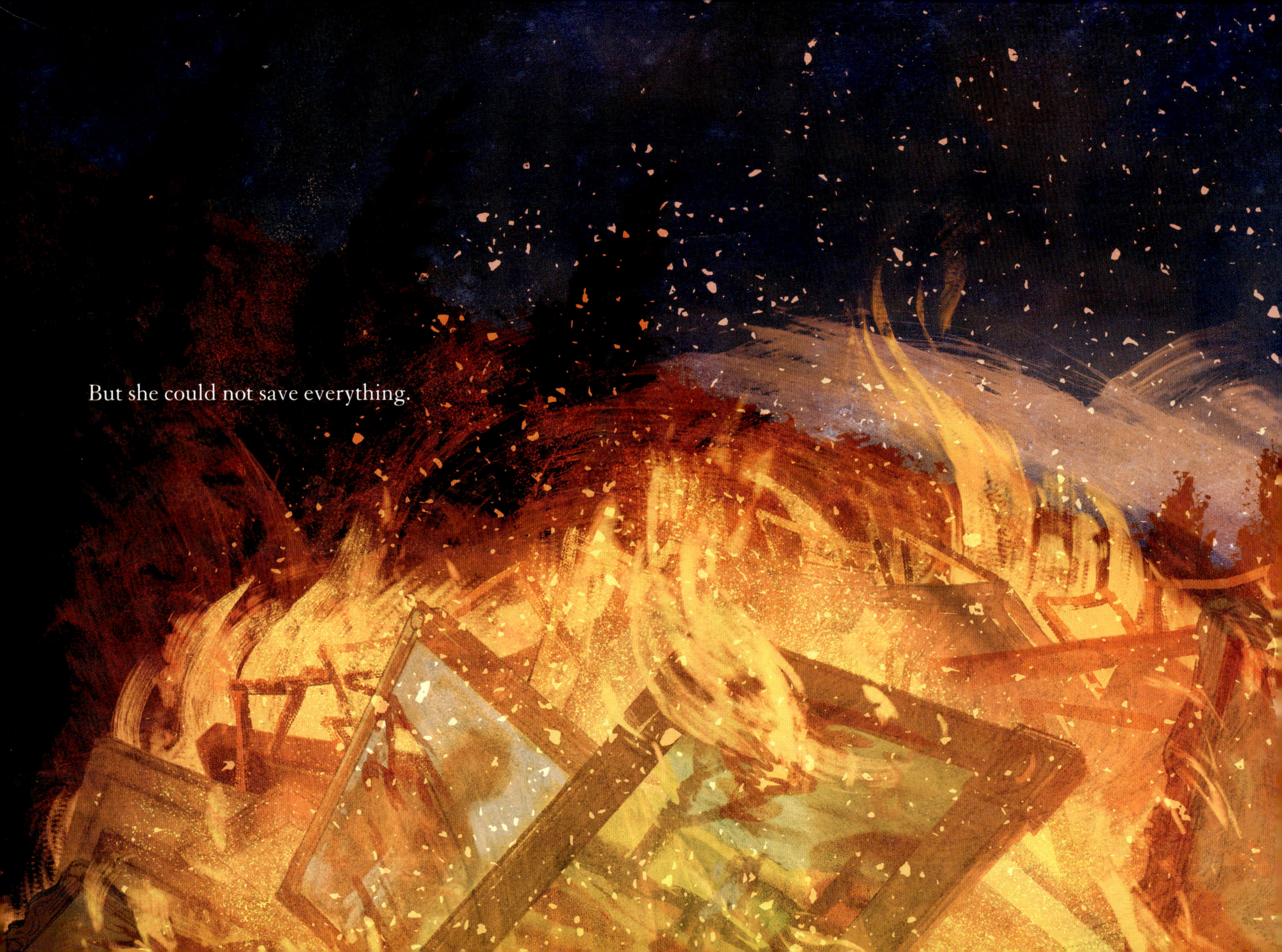

But she could not save everything.

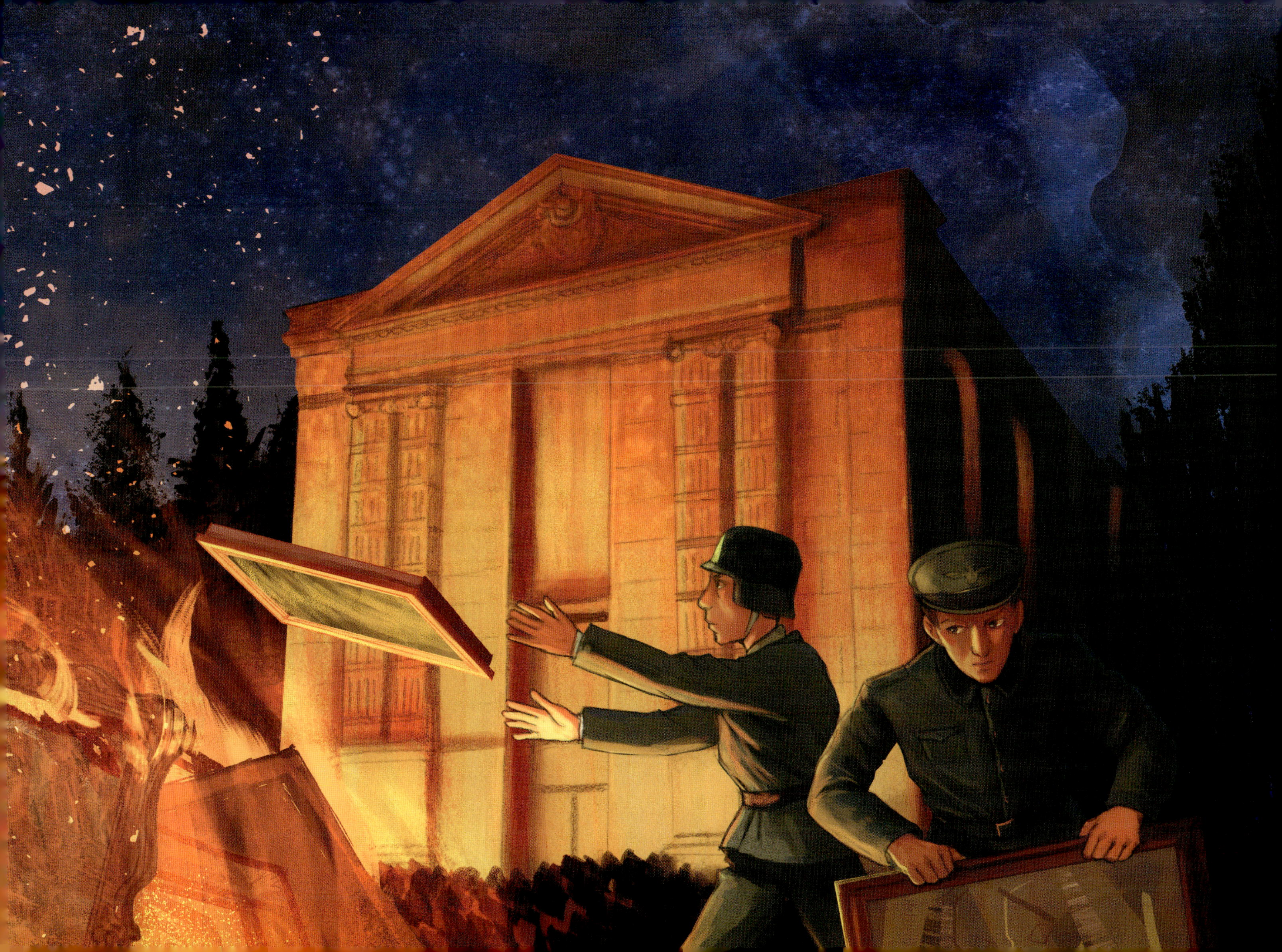

Rose was heartbroken, but she would not give up hope. And elsewhere, the tide was turning. The war had reached a critical point—it looked as though Paris would once again be free.

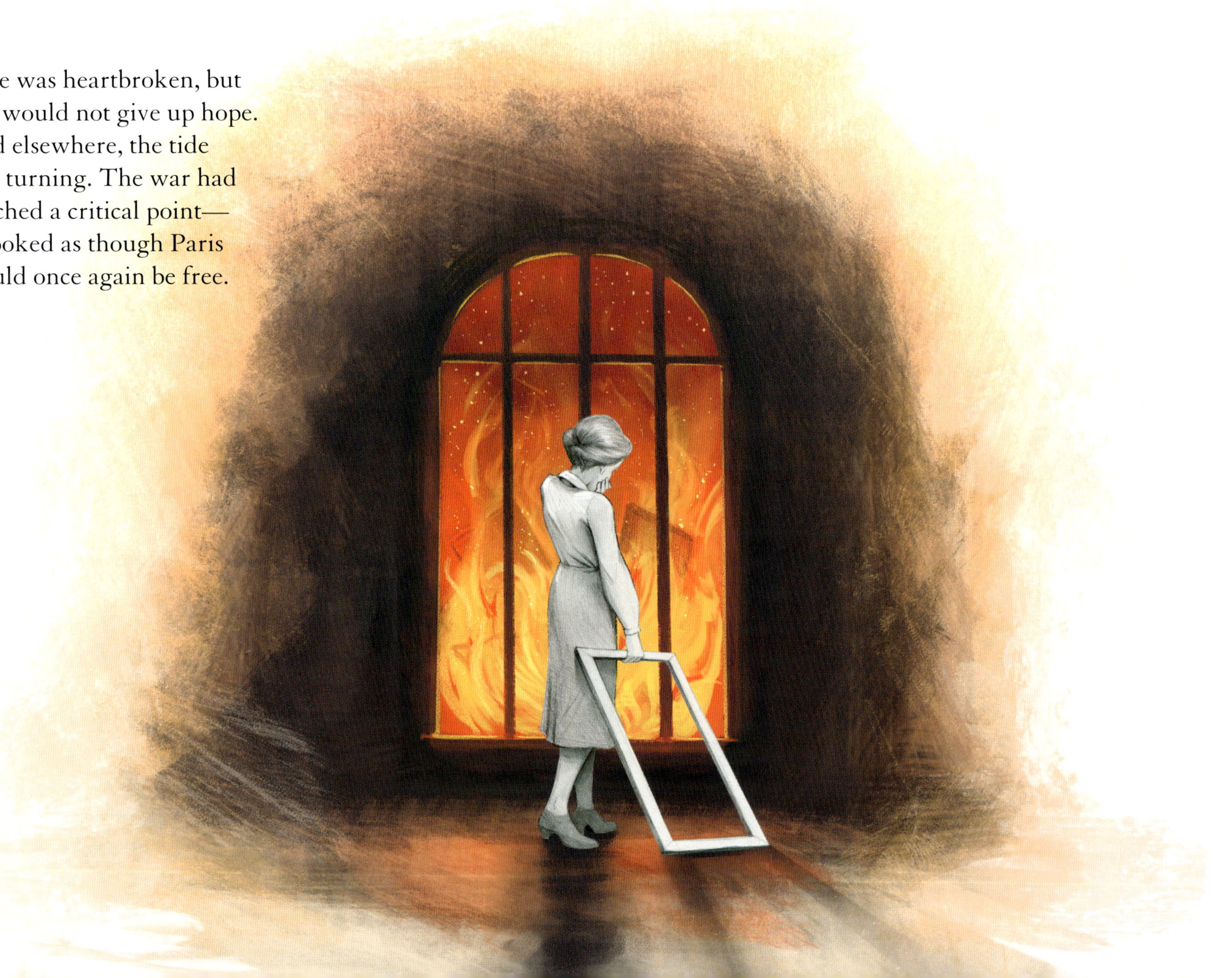

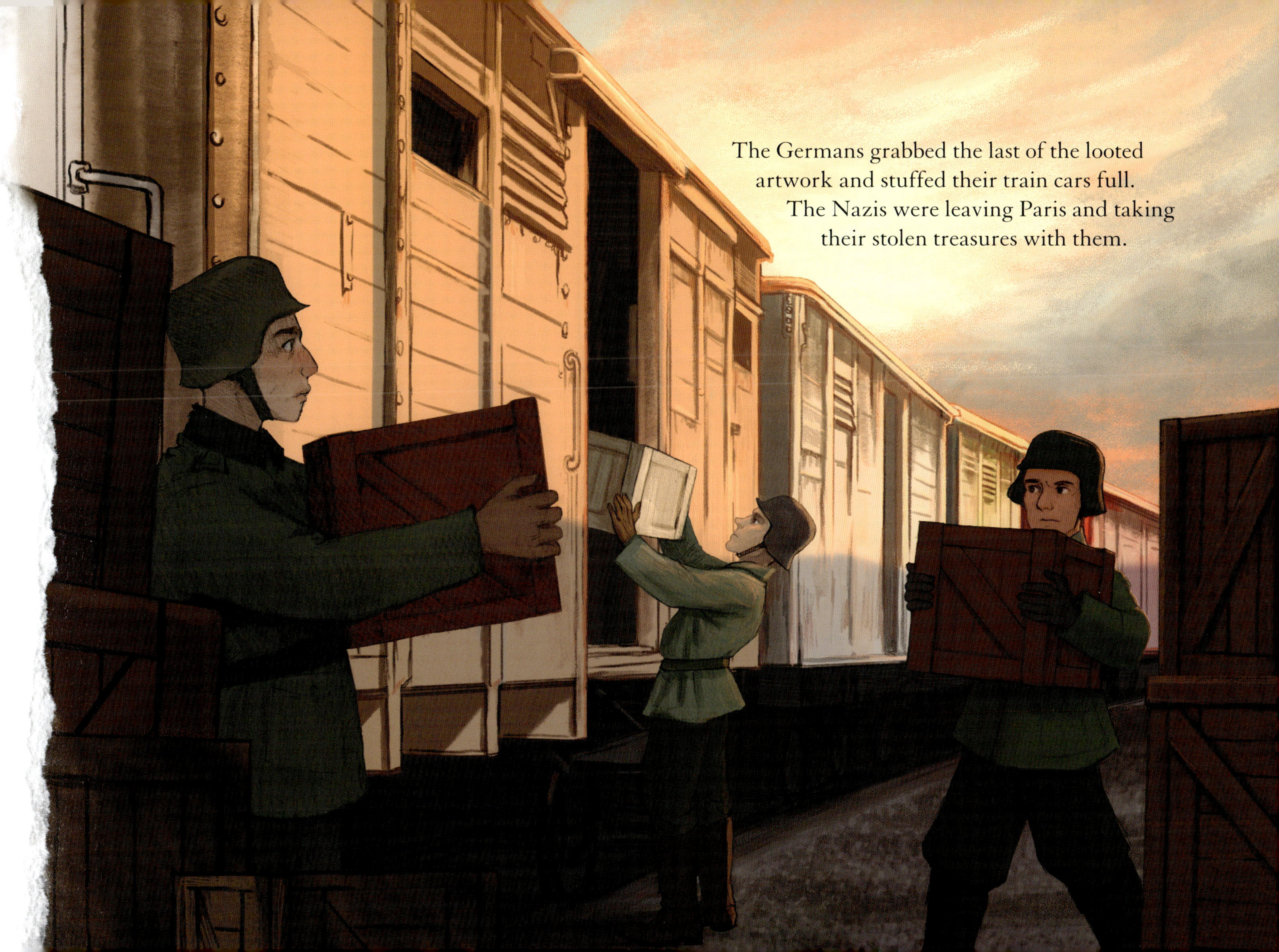

The Germans grabbed the last of the looted artwork and stuffed their train cars full.

The Nazis were leaving Paris and taking their stolen treasures with them.

Rose knew which trains held the artwork.
She knew where the trains were going.

Now was not the time to be quiet.
Now was not the time to listen.

Now she had to act.

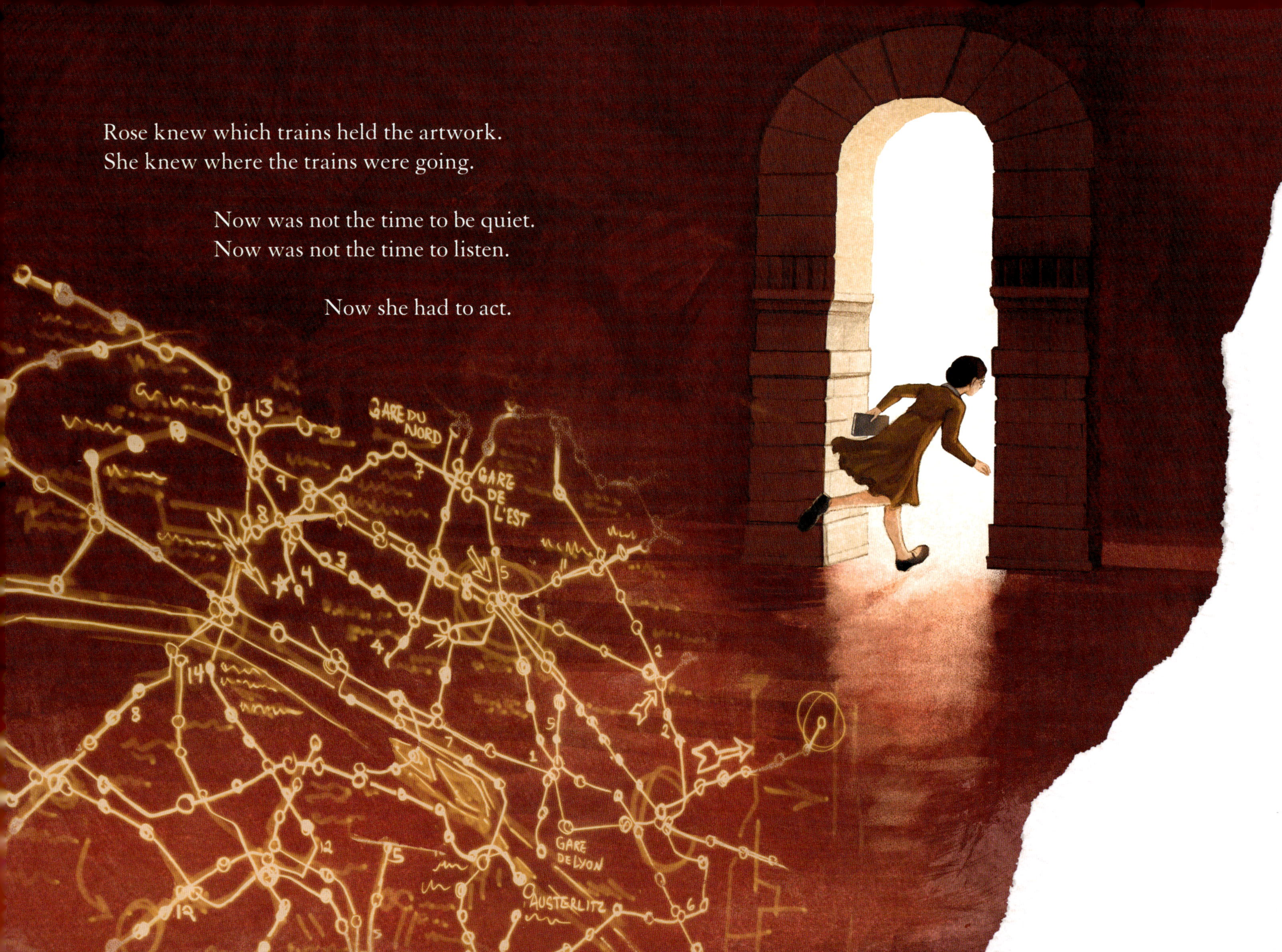

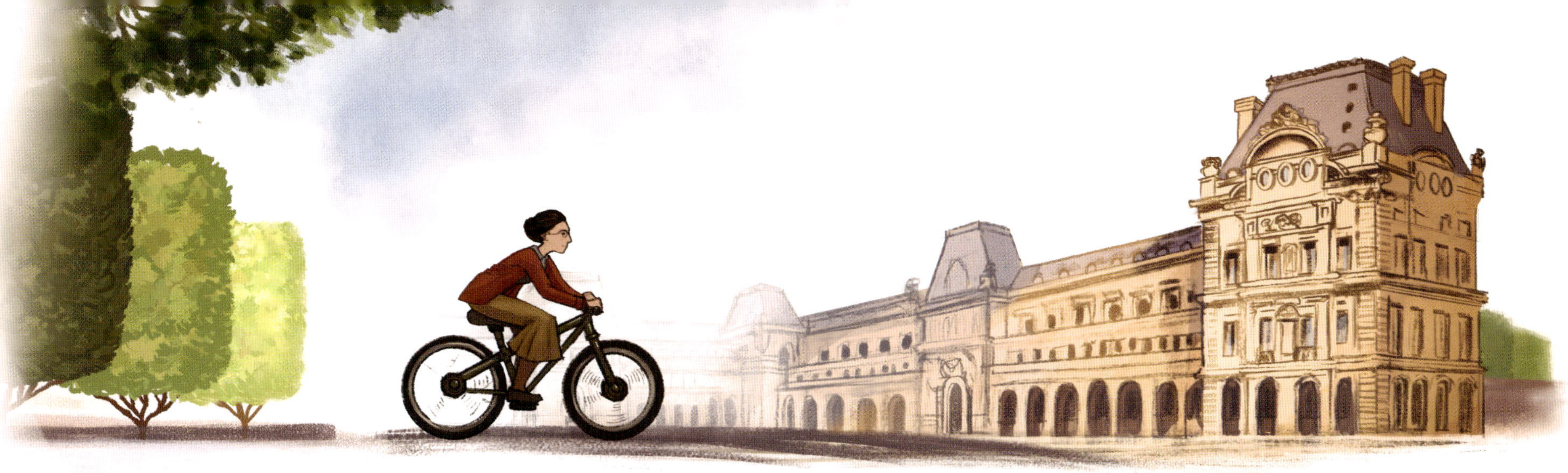

She sent word to the French Resistance and begged them to save their country's treasures.

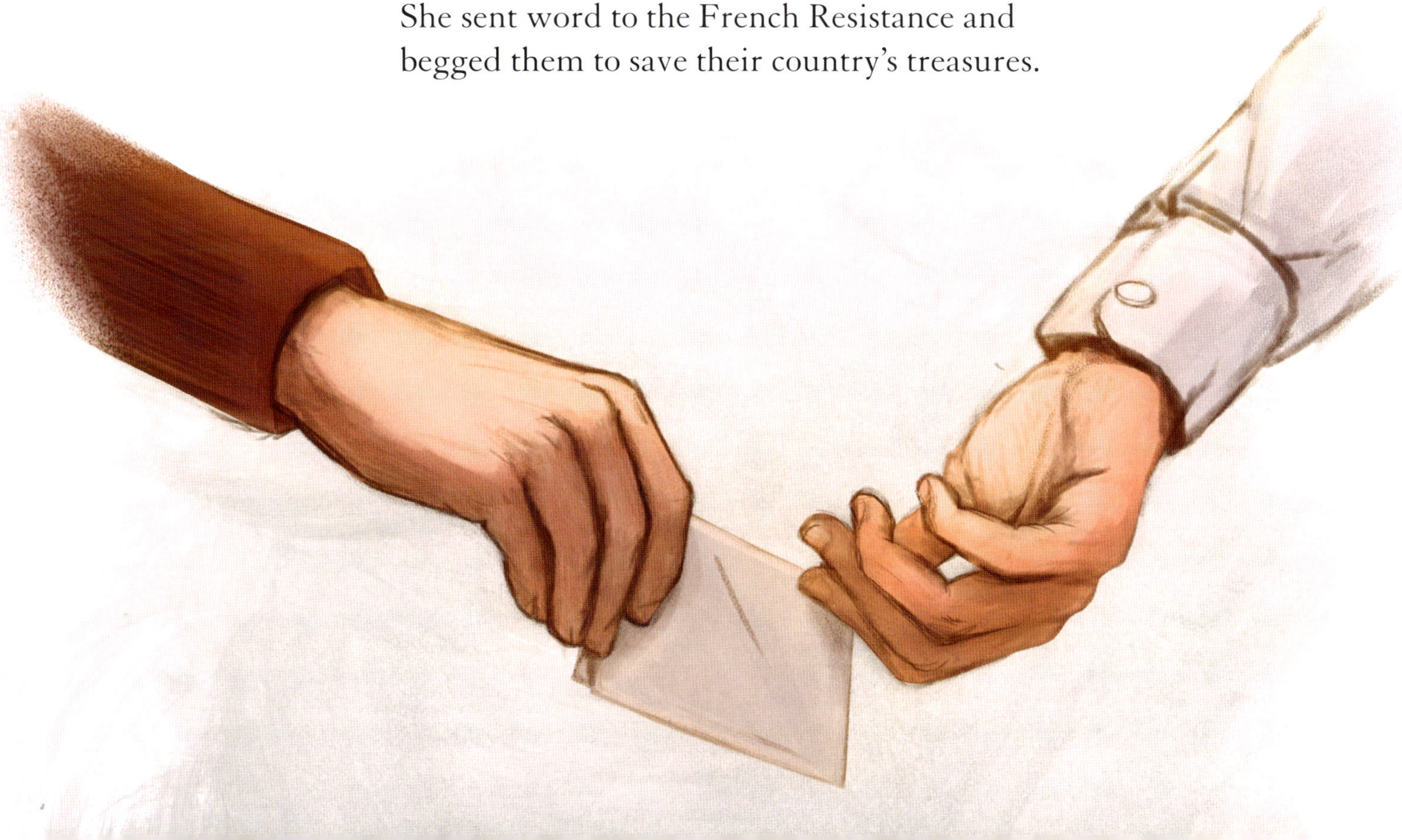

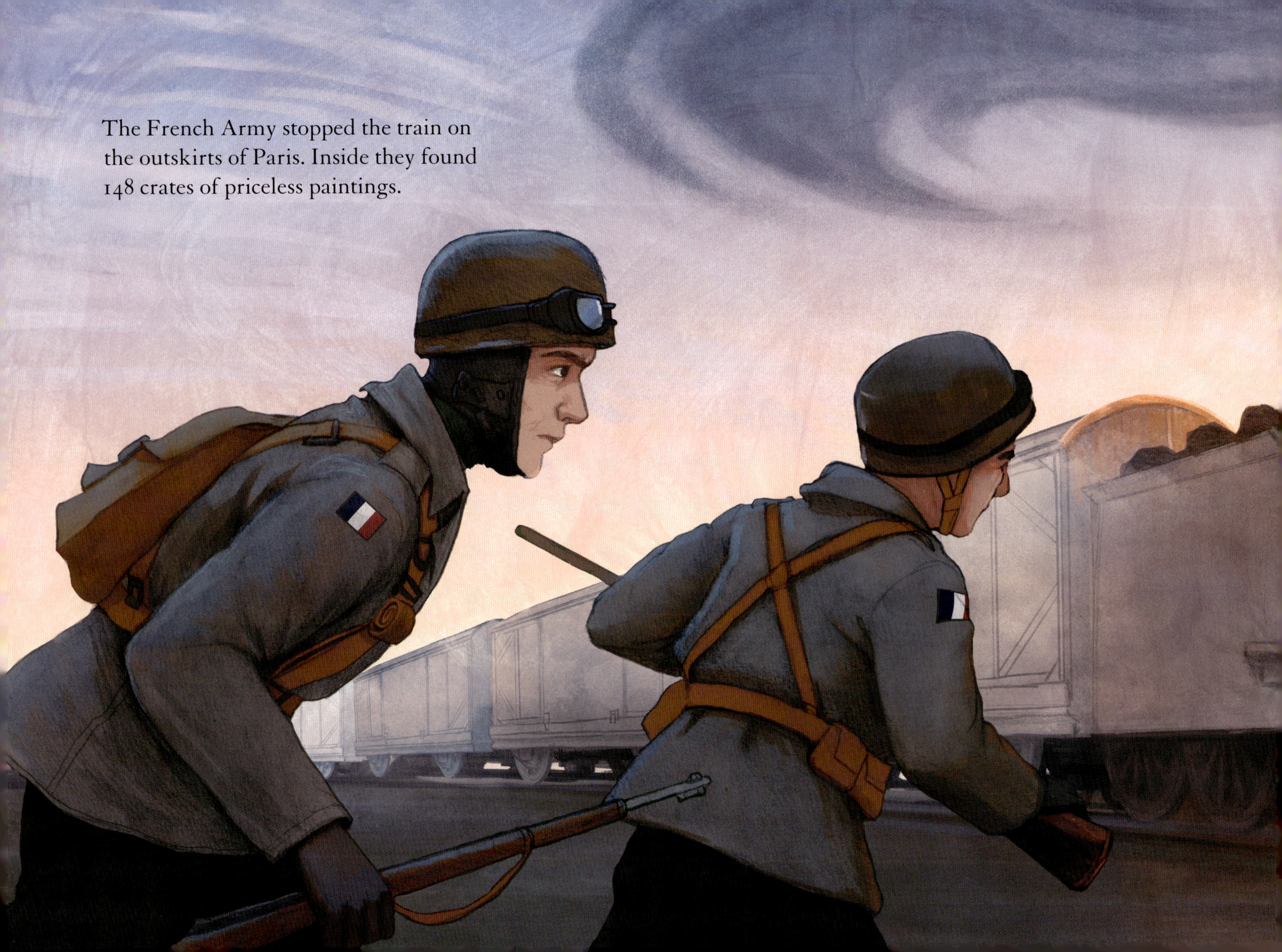

The French Army stopped the train on the outskirts of Paris. Inside they found 148 crates of priceless paintings.

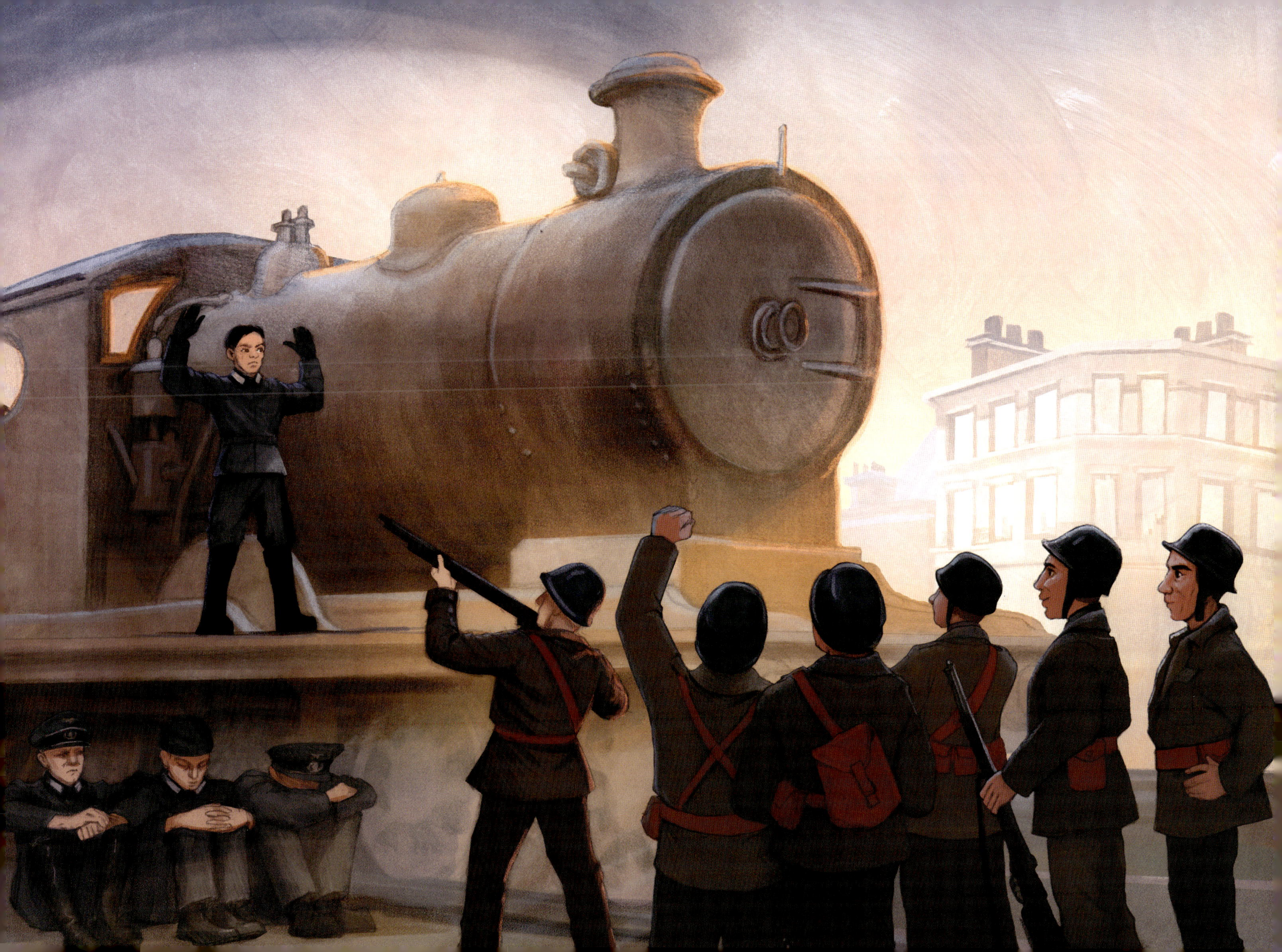

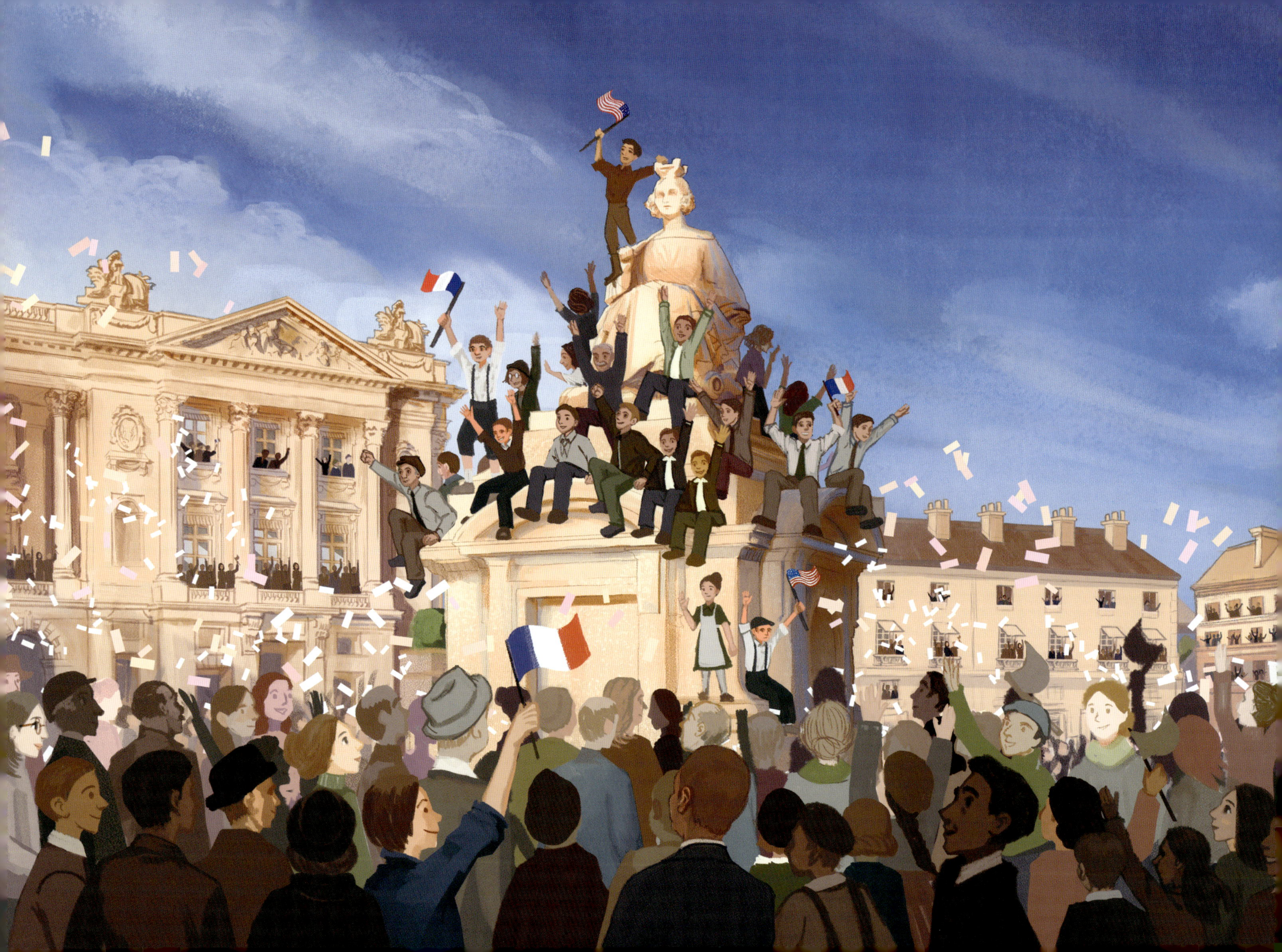

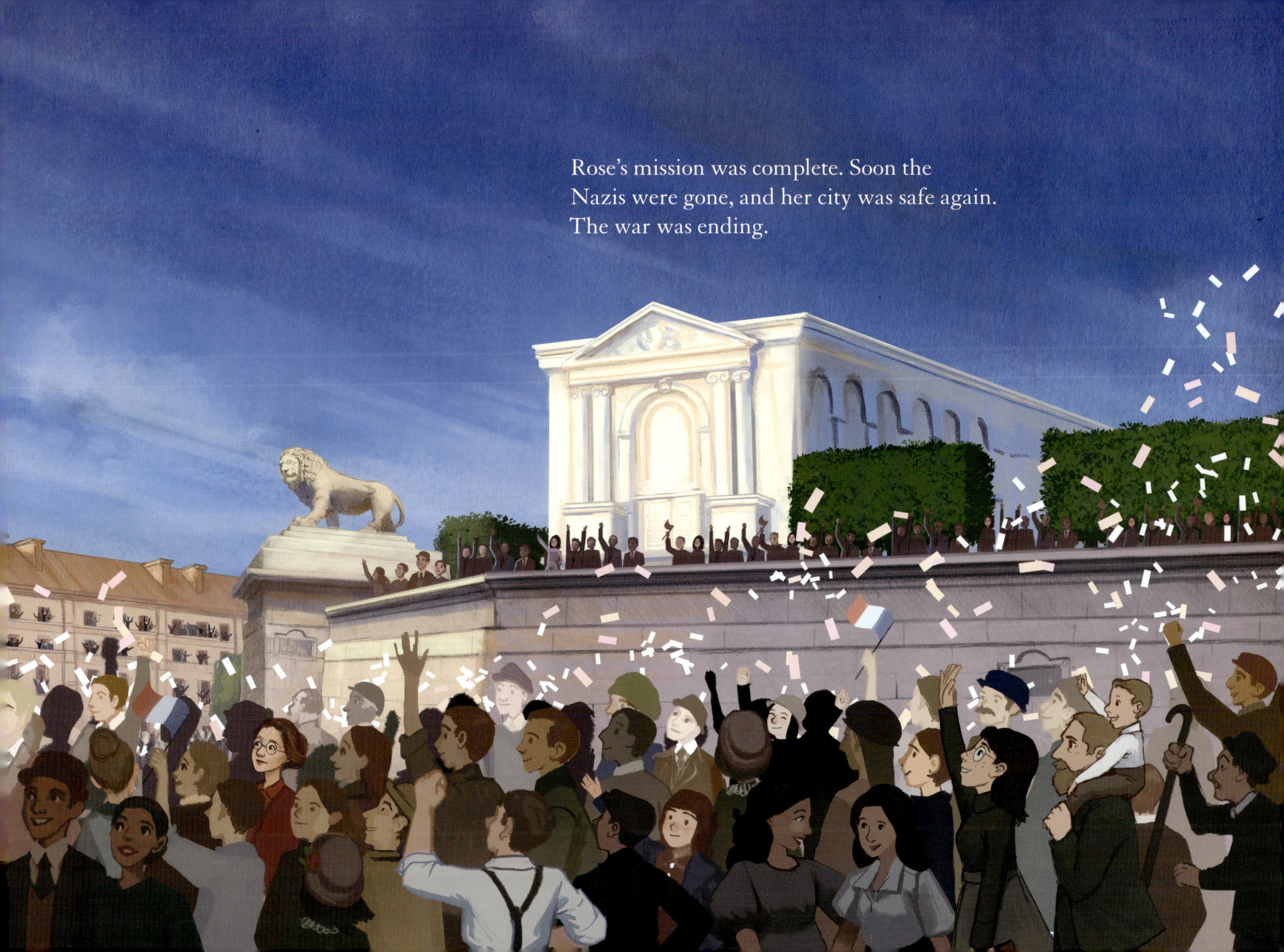

Rose's mission was complete. Soon the Nazis were gone, and her city was safe again. The war was ending.

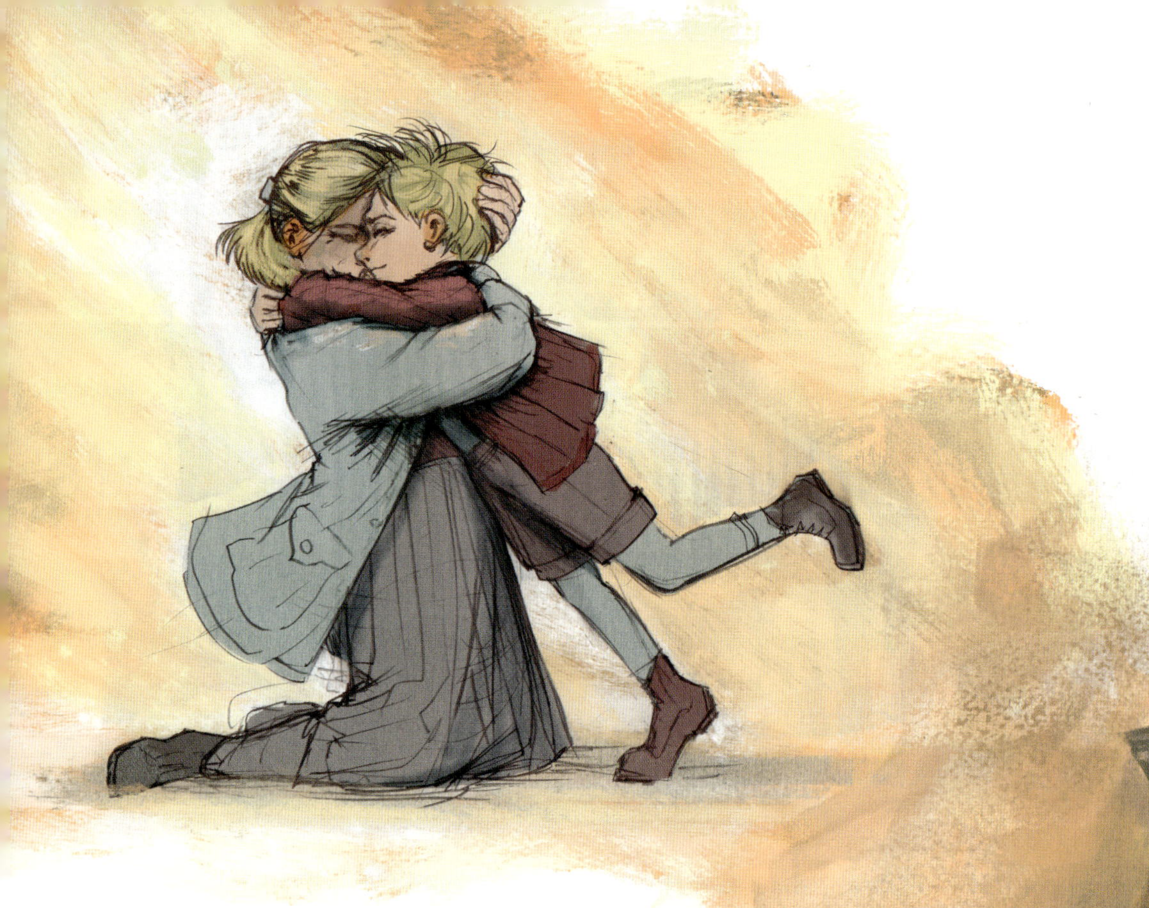

But even as the armies retreated, as cities were rebuilt, as families reunited, thousands of works of art were still missing.

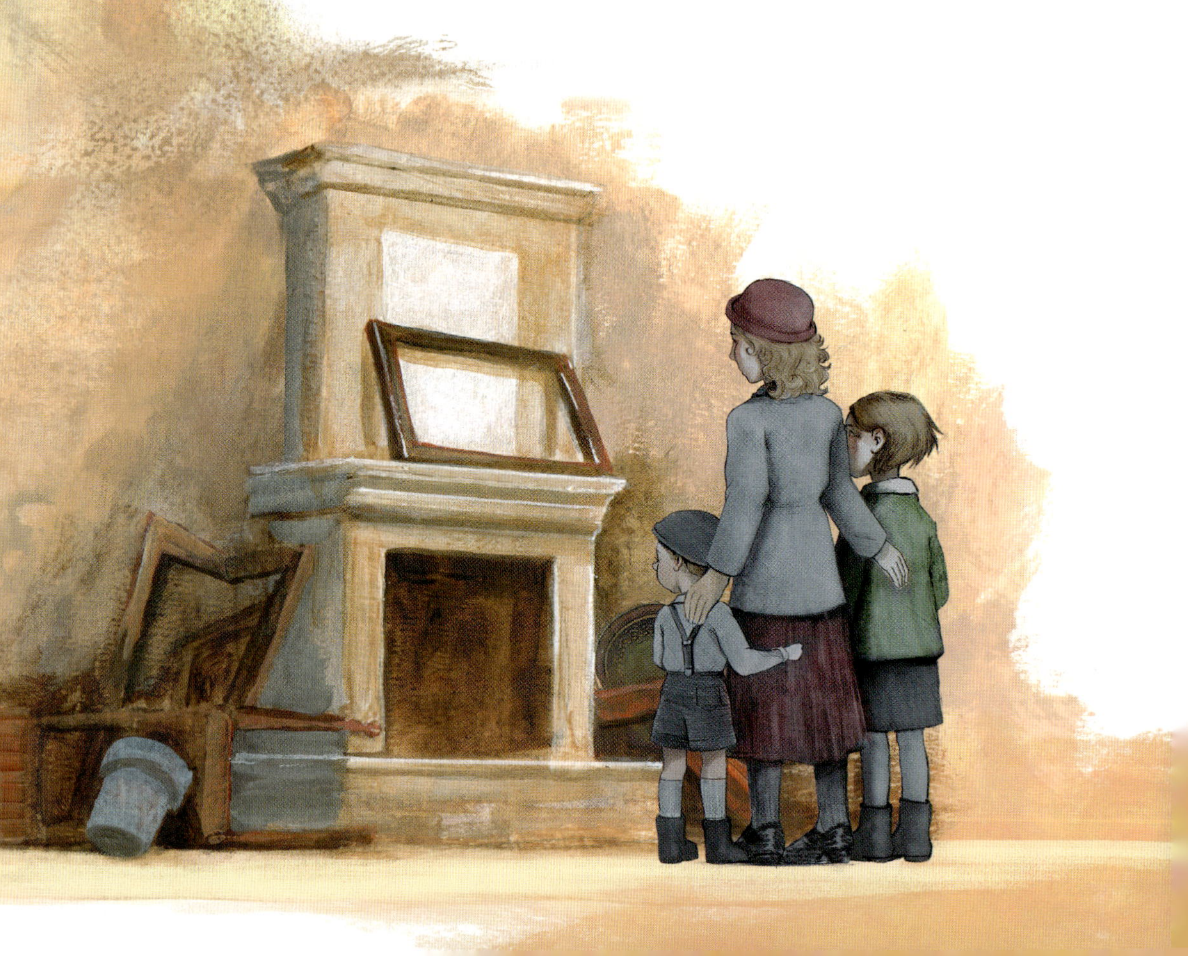

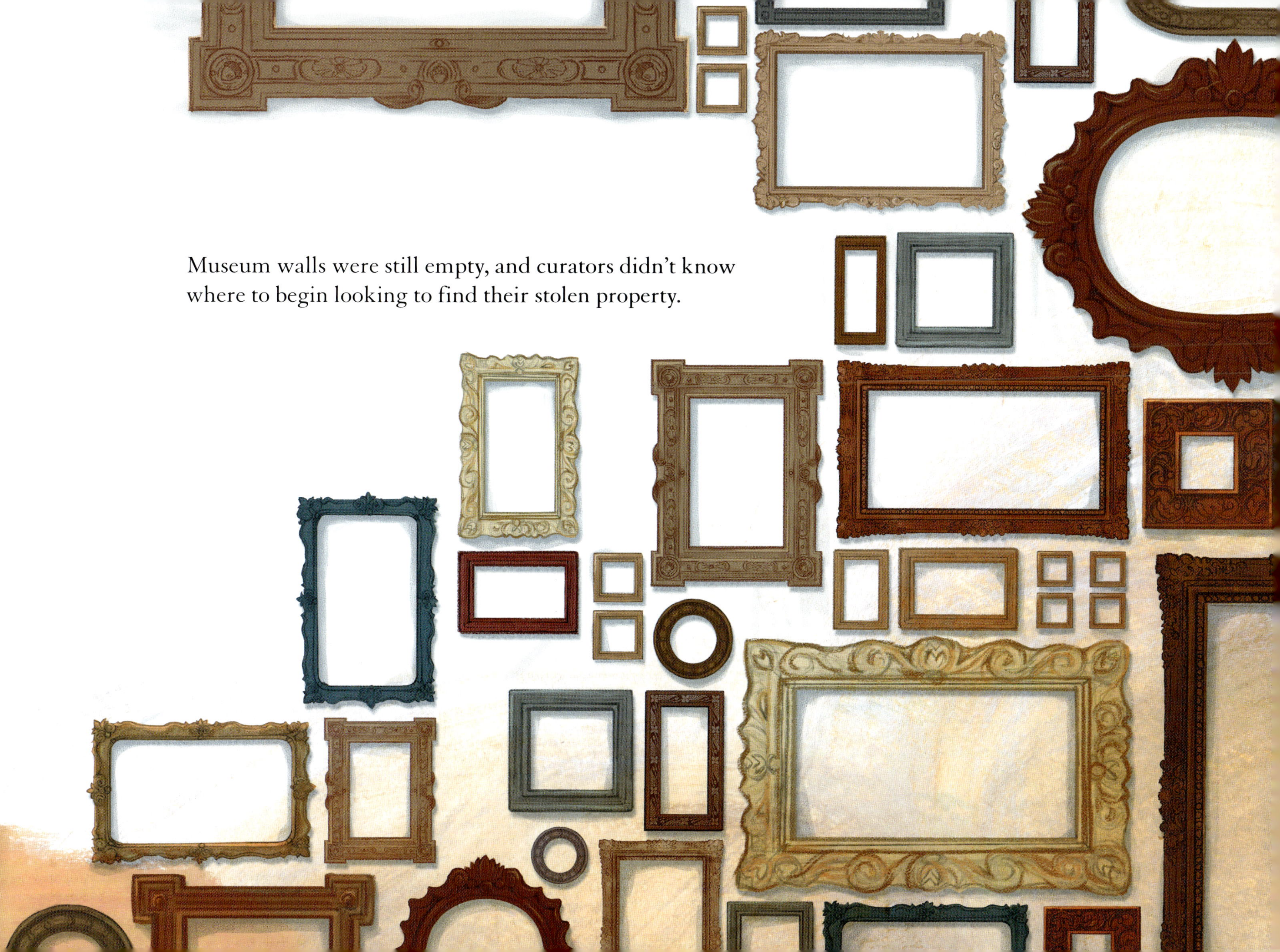

Museum walls were still empty, and curators didn’t know where to begin looking to find their stolen property.

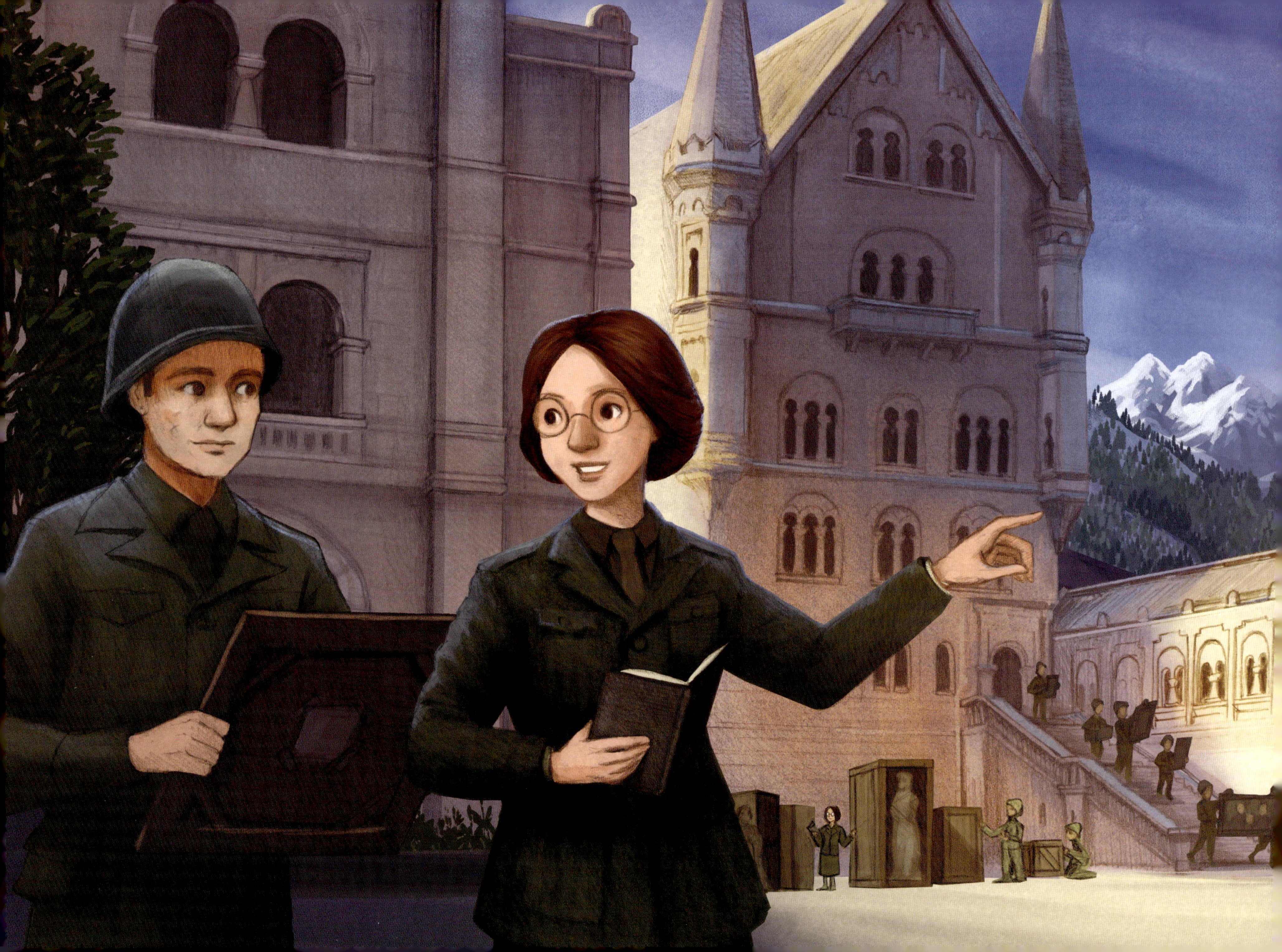

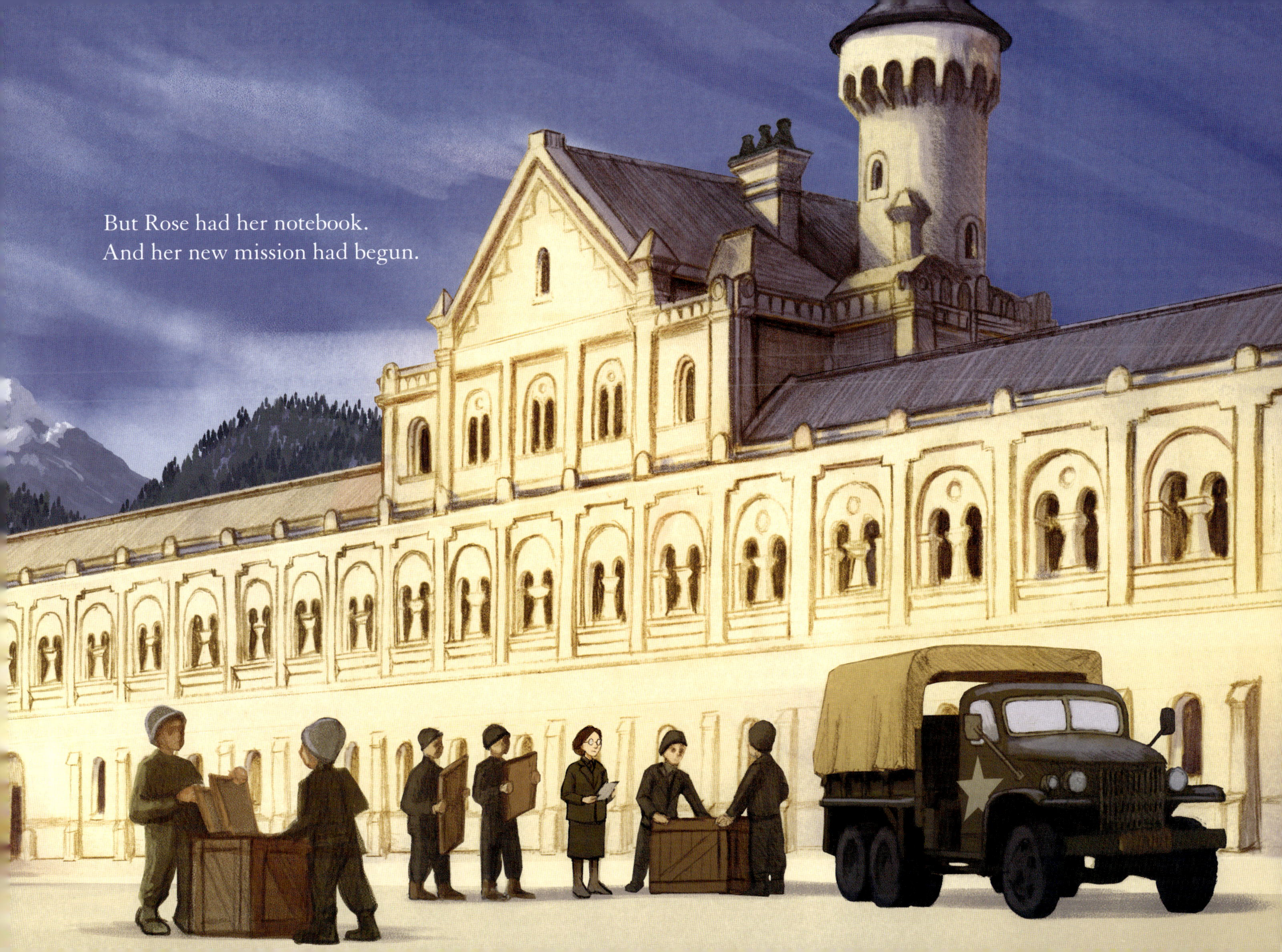

But Rose had her notebook.
And her new mission had begun.

Historical Note

The scale of the Nazis' art theft operation in Europe during World War II was enormous. But so were Rose Valland's spy efforts in Paris. By the time the war ended in 1945, she had secretly recorded the locations of twenty thousand works of art that had passed through the Jeu de Paume alone.

Rose's mission after the war turned from spying to restitution—returning the stolen artwork to its rightful owners. She devoted years to sorting and returning works to museums as well as to the Jewish families whose private art collections had been targeted. Her impeccable notes and records kept during the war were critical for this immense task. She had tracked the movement of thousands of paintings, sculptures, rare books, and other valuable cultural items to hoards of Nazi loot all over Europe, and she was responsible for the return of over sixty thousand works of art to the rightful owners.

Rose retired in 1968, but she continued to aid the French restitution effort. For her work during the war, she received France's highest award, the Legion of Honour, as well as one of America's highest awards, the Medal of Freedom.

To this day, thousands of paintings and cultural artifacts are still missing from public and private collections all over Europe.

So the mission continues.

Sources

Bouchoux, Corinne, et al. *Rose Valland: Resistance at the Museum*. Laurel Publishing, 2013.

Edsel, Robert M., and Bret Witter. *The Monuments Men: Allied Heroes, Nazi Thieves, and the Greatest Treasure Hunt in History*. New York: Little, Brown, 2009.

Nicholas, Lynn H. *The Rape of Europa: The Fate of Europe's Treasures in the Third Reich and the Second World War*. New York: Knopf, 1994.

Polack, Emmanuelle, and Philippe Dagen. *Les carnets de Rose Valland: Le pillage des collections privées d'œuvres d'art en France durant la Seconde Guerre Mondiale*. Lyon: Fage, 2011.

Riding, Alan. *And the Show Went On: Cultural Life in Nazi-Occupied Paris*. New York: Vintage, 2010.

Valland, Rose. *Le front de l'art. Défense des collections Françaises, 1939-1945*. Paris: RMN, 1961.

Author's Note

My grandfather Robert McInnis served in the US Army during World War II. When he returned home, he used the GI Bill to pay for art school. He would go on to become my unofficial first art teacher, patiently showing me how to draw faces and cartoon characters. Through him, I was exposed to both art and history. When we're young, history can sometimes feel so removed from our experiences, but for me, my grandfather was a living connection to that history.

I first learned of Rose Valland when I was a college student studying illustration. There are many stories of small, overlooked acts of heroism from WWII, but Rose's story is different, because in addition to helping people through her reporting to the French Resistance, her main effort was to save artwork. She risked her life for years, showing up to her museum again and again, even though she knew the risks.

Why does it matter to protect art? I've spent a long time researching Rose against the backdrop of other modern-day cultural shifts. Censorship, book banning, even the destruction of books, all helped me realize that the question is not "Why does it matter to protect art?" but rather "Why did it matter to the Nazis to destroy it?" They were not just destroying meaningless paint, canvas, and paper, but the ideas themselves. They were trying to tell entire societies that these ideas did not deserve to flourish and persevere. During the 1930s and 1940s, the world was becoming an increasingly connected place. Artists were creating works that challenged old ideas and showed a world that was more diverse, vibrant, and interesting than any of us could have imagined and that a wide variety of people deserved a place in our collective human creativity.

Beyond the material wealth that Rose helped to recover, she protected those ideas. She matters in the same way that today's librarians, authors, and publishers matter. She couldn't save everything, but she did what she could.

Acknowledgments

This book was an incredible labor of love. I'd like to thank Andrew Olson, Marianne McGuire, Griffin Olson, and the rest of my family for their support. Thank you to Susan Cohen, who shepherded this book in the early stages and helped me find a home for Rose's story. Thank you to Michael McCartney and Allyn Johnston at Beach Lane for all of their expertise and care in bringing this story to life and for their incredible patience as I illustrated this book during a pandemic—with a newborn. And thank you to my art families, from my Ringling teachers and friends to my Hartford MFA crew. Thank you all.

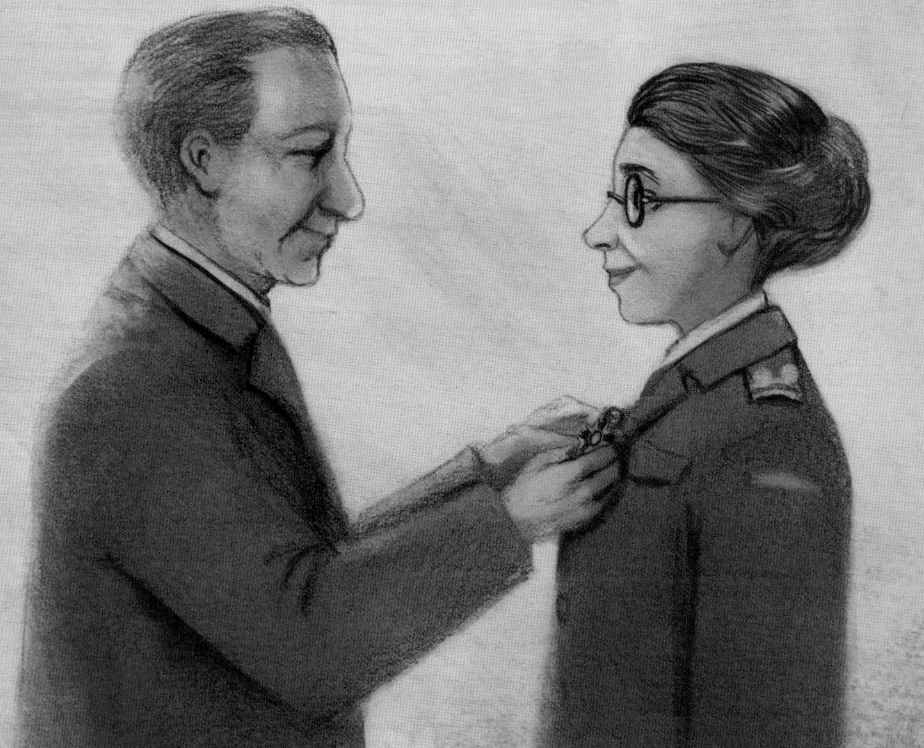

For Griffin Olson

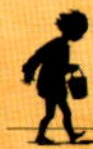

BEACH LANE BOOKS · An imprint of Simon & Schuster Children's Publishing Division · 1230 Avenue of the Americas, New York, New York 10020 · For more than 100 years, Simon & Schuster has championed authors and the stories they create. By respecting the copyright of an author's intellectual property, you enable Simon & Schuster and the author to continue publishing exceptional books for years to come. We thank you for supporting the author's copyright by purchasing an authorized edition of this book. · For information about special discounts for bulk purchases, please contact Simon & Schuster Special Sales at 1-866-506-1949 or business@simonandschuster.com. · Simon & Schuster strongly believes in freedom of expression and stands against censorship in all its forms. For more information, visit BooksBelong.com. · The Simon & Schuster Speakers Bureau can bring authors to your live event. For more information or to book an event, contact the Simon & Schuster Speakers Bureau at 1-866-248-3049 or visit our website at www.simonspeakers.com. · The text for this book was set in Granjon LT. · The illustrations for this book were drawn in graphite and mixed media and painted digitally. · Manufactured in China · 0525 SCP · First Edition · 1 2 3 4 5 6 7 8 9 10 · Library of Congress Cataloging-in-Publication Data · Names: McGuire, Erin, author. · Title: The spy in the museum : how Rose Valland saved art from the Nazis / Erin McGuire. · Description: First edition. | New York : Beach Lane Books, [2025] | Audience: Ages 6–10 | Audience: Grades 2–3 | Summary: "This biography tells the true story of Rose Valland's valiant efforts to save thousands of works of art during World War II by doing the only thing she could: Becoming a spy in her own museum"—Provided by publisher. · Identifiers: LCCN 2024045300 (print) | LCCN 2024045301 (ebook) | ISBN 9781534466173 (hardcover) | ISBN 9781534466180 (ebook) · Subjects: LCSH: Valland, Rose—Juvenile literature. | Musée du jeu de paume (France)—Juvenile literature. | Art treasures in war—France—History—20th century—Juvenile literature. | World War, 1939-1945—Art and the war—Juvenile literature. | World War, 1939-1945—Destruction and pillage—France—Juvenile literature. | World War, 1939-1945—Underground movements—France—Juvenile literature. | France—History—German occupation, 1940-1945—Juvenile literature. | Art museum curators—France—Paris—Biography. | World War, 1939-1945—Confiscations and contributions—Germany—Biography. | Spies—France—Biography. · Classification: LCC N9165.F8 V356 2025 (print) | LCC N9165.F8 (ebook) | DDC 940.53/1—dc23/eng/20241107 · LC record available at https://lccn.loc.gov/2024045300 · LC ebook record available at https://lccn.loc.gov/2024045301

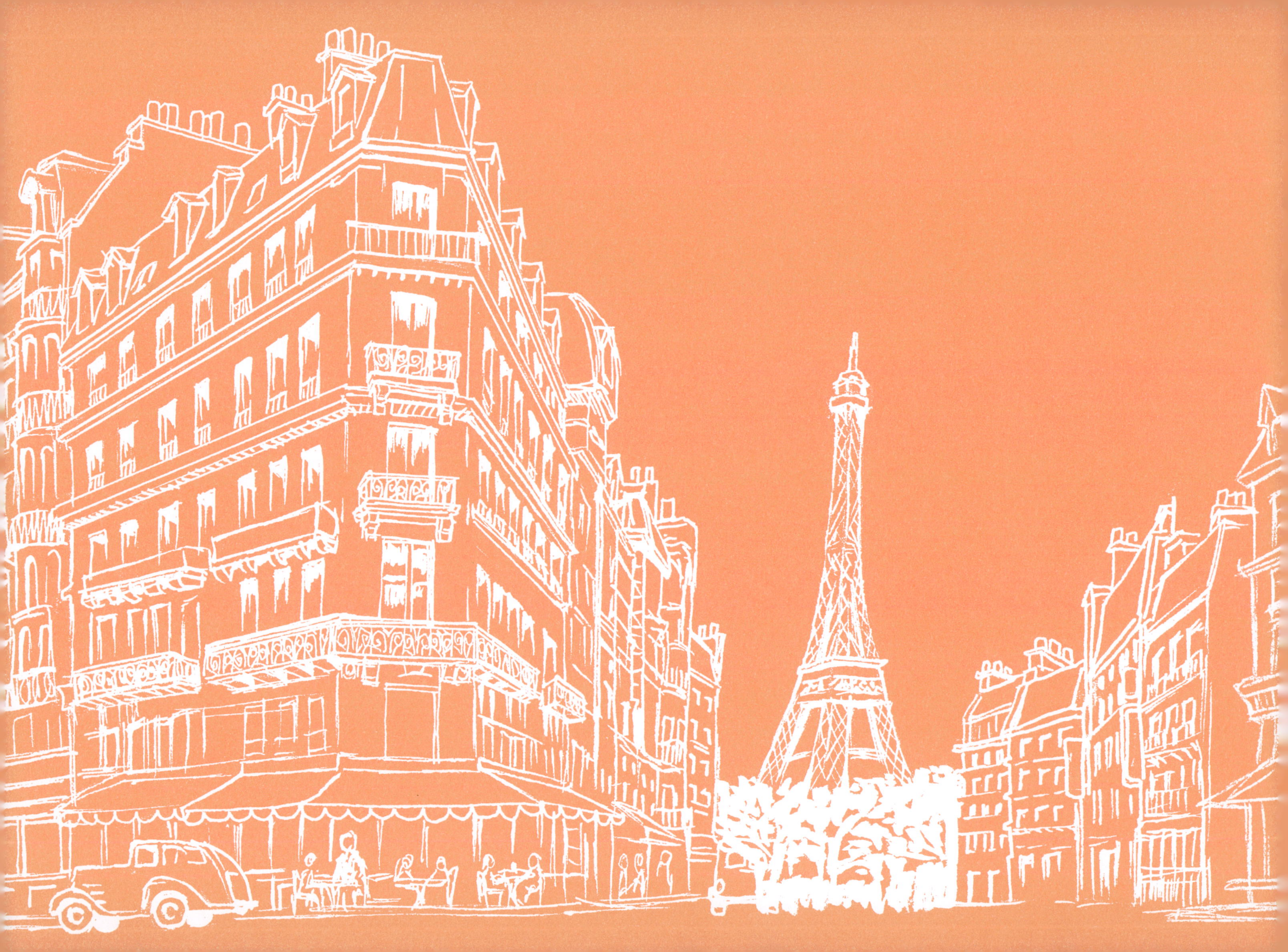